What stands out?
Connections?
Remember: youth confinement,
Constraint, and Resistance

HUMAN TARGETS

HUMAN TARGETS

Schools, Police, and
the Criminalization
of Latino Youth

VICTOR M. RIOS

Foreword by James Diego Vigil

THE UNIVERSITY OF CHICAGO PRESS
CHICAGO AND LONDON

The University of Chicago Press, Chicago 60637
The University of Chicago Press, Ltd., London
© 2017 by The University of Chicago
All rights reserved. No part of this book may be used or reproduced in any manner
whatsoever without written permission, except in the case of brief quotations
in critical articles and reviews. For more information, contact the University of
Chicago Press, 1427 E. 60th St., Chicago, IL 60637.
Published 2017.
Printed in the United States of America

26 25 24 23 22 21 20 19 18 17   1 2 3 4 5

ISBN-13: 978-0-226-09085-6 (cloth)
ISBN-13: 978-0-226-09099-3 (paper)
ISBN-13: 978-0-226-09104-4 (e-book)
DOI: 10.7208/chicago/9780226091044.001.0001

Library of Congress Cataloging-in-Publication Data

Names: Rios, Victor M., author. | Vigil, James Diego, 1938– writer of foreword.
Title: Human targets : schools, police, and the criminalization of Latino youth /
Victor M. Rios.
Description: Chicago ; London : The University of Chicago Press, 2017. |
Includes bibliographical references and index.
Identifiers: LCCN 2016032600 | ISBN 9780226090856 (cloth : alk. paper) |
ISBN 9780226090993 (pbk. : alk. paper) | ISBN 9780226091044 (e-book)
Subjects: LCSH: Juvenile delinquents—California—Social conditions. |
Gang members—California—Social conditions. | Hispanic American youth—
California—Social conditions. | Gang members—California—Attitudes. | Juvenile
delinquents—California—Attitudes. | Hispanic American youth—California—
Attitudes. | Police-community relations. | Intergroup relations. | Teacher-student
relationships. | Interpersonal relations.
Classification: LCC HV9104 .R56 2017 | DDC 364.36089/680794—dc23
LC record available at https://lccn.loc.gov/2016032600

♾ This paper meets the requirements of ANSI/NISO Z39.48–1992
(Permanence of Paper).

CONTENTS

FOREWORD

One of the recurring debates in social science research is whether a native, insider perspective provides a fuller, more accurate picture of a social group. In contrast, the outsider gaze maintains that distance makes for objectivity and helps avoid the ethical and political biases that plague researchers that are feeling too much about what they see and hear. What makes Victor Rios's work so forceful and interesting is that he has succeeded in doing both. His work is an insider-outsider mix that brings authenticity to his ethnographic work of seeing and hearing street youth. He also provides a wider, broader canvas to utilize what other researchers see and hear. In other words, he combines his subjective close-ups with wide-angle insights compiled as he navigates between his insider/outsider status. Like the youths in his book who are constantly shifting between personae and identities, he has developed a methodology that teaches us to frame switch in order to understand the social phenomenon at hand.

Human Targets demonstrates and clarifies how public authorities such as the police and schools overstep their bounds, indeed their charge, by negatively and characteristically hounding and pounding gang youths. It also shows the complexity of identities that gang members develop as they lurch through a crazy maze set and structured through generations of racial prejudice and persistent poverty. For too long, the storyline has been in one direction: gangs are bad, and they do bad things because they are bad people. *Human Targets* will augment that line of reasoning by pointing out that certainly some gangs are bad and have some gang members doing bad things but the bad can also stem from and be created or fueled by other social institutions and authority figures, notably police and schools.

This book defies the insider-outsider, subjective-objective, native–going native, qualitative-quantitative contrasts and debates and pushes us to learn about the consequences of the punitive treatment, such as harsh school discipline or police harassment and brutality, that we impose on marginalized children. In the end, we are left understanding that in order to develop solutions for the complex problems that marginalized youths face, we must develop nuanced studies that help to illuminate the fully complex lives that young people live, the multifarious cultures they utilize, and the ways in which society has come to govern them by belligerently regulating their behaviors, frames, and worldviews.

James Diego Vigil

Crossing
Institutional
Settings

The foul-tasting latex flavor of the blueberry-sized, heroin-filled balloons tucked inside my bottom lip forced me to compulsively spit, leaving a trail of saliva splotches on the sidewalk to evaporate in the hot California sun. After my homeboy and business partner, Conejo, and I shared a forty-ounce bottle of Olde English malt liquor, I had saved the bottle to fill with water from any functioning outdoor faucet I could find in this precarious corner of East Oakland— Twenty-Seventh Avenue and Foothill Boulevard. Sometimes, I added a packet of bright-red, cherry Kool-Aid to give the water some flavor.

Fifteen years old and desperate for money in 1993, I teamed up with Conejo to find a new venture. Conejo was in his early twenties and had sold heroin here in the past. Feeling left out of the education process, I had dropped out of school. We each invested twenty-five dollars to purchase a caramel-chew-sized chunk of heroin, which we broke into ten smaller pieces to sell for ten dollars each. We sealed each piece in small water balloons to hide inside our mouths; if the police stopped and frisked us, we could swallow the balloons. Later, we figured, we could dig through our excrement and recover the goods. This was risky business, and we knew it: Two of our homies had been hospitalized from ingesting heroine that had leaked into their intestines after they had swallowed their balloons. But for Conejo and me, selling heroin was both a desperate way to earn some money and bold proof of our manhood on the streets—we were self-sufficient and could handle danger. Through our industrious entre-

Perhaps to
Narrator & Conejo's
reform (?) they
Selling drugs was
of new start and
could force

preneurship, we could gain self-worth, belonging, dignity, pride,
and cash—the very resources that social institutions made unat-
tainable for poor youth like us. Conejo and I thought we had found a
way to make something out of nothing, to persist, to survive—or in
the words of our elders who had taught us about survival and hard
work, *buscando vida*—loosely translated, "in search of livelihood."
This hard-work ethic had entered the informal economy with us.

The next step was to test the product. We couldn't risk retaliation
for poisoning someone with a bad batch. A few local *tecatos*—heroin
addicts—were more than willing to offer their services: free heroin
testing in exchange for free product. With few words between us
besides a *q-vo*, "what's up," Topo, one of the addicts, gestured with
his head in the direction of Sausal Creek, and we followed him half
a block away to the dry creek bed. With an index finger, I scooped
one of the balloons from inside my bottom lip, wiped it dry on my
black, extra-baggy Ben Davis work pants, and handed it to Topo. He
ripped it open, pinched off a piece of the gooey, black tar heroin, and
placed it on a tarnished, stainless-steel spoon that he pulled from
his pocket. Topo asked for some of the bright-red Kool-Aid from my
bottle. I looked at him with a puzzled face.

"It'll give it good flavor, homie!" he muttered.[1]

I poured a bit of the drink in the bottle cap and transferred it into
the spoon. With a lighter, Topo heated the spoon from the bottom,
and the lump of heroin melted into a *caldito*, "little soup." Carefully,
Topo handed the spoon to Conejo to hold as he grabbed a syringe
from his pocket and filled it with the *caldito*. He wrapped a red bandana around his arm, forcefully smacked his wrist with two fingers,
and injected himself.

"Please don't die. . . . I wanna make some money," I thought to myself.

Less than a minute later, Topo turned to us from his squatted
position, and flashed a big smile. In a languid tone, he whispered,
" *'Ta bueno*" (it's good).

"Hell, yeah! We finna make some money!" I wanted to shout, but
I slowly nodded, playing it cool.

Grinding heroin for two fourteen-hour days on street corners waiting for clients yielded a profit of fifty dollars. I had doubled my initial investment, but the glamour of drug-selling quickly turned into a scary reality. I couldn't shake the fear of getting caught, becoming addicted, or ending up in prison. The possibility of being victimized and perpetually stuck making low wages loomed large. I knew a handful of guys who made hundreds of dollars a day selling drugs, but the majority of us hit a "tar ceiling" at street-level dealing, with very little money trickling down our way. Fear of the short-term consequences—violence or arrest—was enough, and I was blind to the long-term impact of crime, consequences serious enough to impede my success in adulthood.

After three days of street peddling heroin, a twenty-something-year-old veteran drug dealer approached me as I leaned against a wall on the back side of the liquor store where Conejo, a half-dozen other guys, and I usually posted, waiting for customers. I was sipping from my bottle of Kool-Aid when he addressed me point-blank, "Why you perpetrating, mothafucka?" Before I could ask him what he was talking about, he smacked the bottle out of my hand, glass shattering against the wall, staining the dingy, khaki-colored paint red. "Get the fuck out of here! If I see you around here again, I'ma scrape your ass, mothafucka!"

"Man, fuck you! You know who I'm with?" I snarled.

He reached into his pants at his waistline and pulled out a gun, waving it around. "I don't give a fuck who you wit'! If I see you around here again, you gonna get shot."

I walked away, looking for Conejo. This guy was cleaning up the area, Conejo cautioned, creating his own drug monopoly. "We could bring the homies and take the territory back . . . is it worth it to you? We making enough money to take the risk? To take this fool out?"

Ignoring Conejo's advice, I started a fight a few days later with the older drug dealer's nephew, a kid my age, to retaliate against his uncle's threats. I was walking with two of my friends when I told them, "Hold on!" and I started running toward the kid. I caught him off guard, from behind, in front of another liquor store a few blocks away and began punching and kicking him. As he ran inside the store for refuge, I walked away, proud of my attack.

About thirty minutes later, I was celebrating, laughing and re-counting the sequence of events, when a 1980s Honda Civic slowed down as it approached us on busy Foothill Boulevard. I turned to see the driver, a chubby-faced, goateed man about forty, look straight at us from behind dark sunglasses. Right below him, I spied the dark-steel and light-wood trim of a shotgun. Instinctually, I fell backward, flat on my ass. A loud shot rang out, followed by a splatter noise as the shotgun shell pelted the wooden steps with dozens of pellet-sized pockmarks less than a foot above my head.

Collapsed on the ground, but uninjured, I sat there alone, my heart pounding. My friends were gone: They had noticed the driver a few seconds ahead of me and managed to jump a nearby fence be-fore the gunshot.

The close call shook me to the core.

At fifteen and no stranger to violence, I had dabbled in marijuana and heroin sales and had stolen bicycles or cars to sell parts for ready cash. None of these activities had produced consistent, lucrative money, and all were fraught with dangers and huge risks. I even had landed in juvenile hall, for felony offenses, and was on strict proba-tionary terms. Mess up again, and I would face some serious time.

But what other choice did I have? I wondered, except to continue to take those risks and face those dangers. What about my dispute with the older drug dealer? Would I step up my game and stake a claim for that street corner? Would I do whatever was necessary to compete with rivals for the territorial rights to sell drugs? And what would happen if I went down that path?

By chance around this time, I found a small flier in my pants pocket that a teacher had given me three weeks ago, the last time I had set foot in school. "Need a Job? Talk to Ms. Miller in Room D211. Fridays at Lunch," the flyer read.

Desperate for cash, I returned to school to pay a visit to Ms. Miller and another teacher, Ms. Russ, who had mentored me in the past and had asked Ms. Miller to look out for me. Ms. Miller, who appeared to like me, made dozens of phone calls to local businesses inquiring about jobs. Finally, German Auto Salvage, an auto repair shop, said they needed someone to clean up the shop four hours a day. It was this or a violent fight for the street corner. So, a few days later, I had a steady job cleaning up a repair shop, dismantling wrecked autos, and helping with oil changes and basic mechanic work. The six-dollar-an-hour wage was more consistent than the money I could earn through the illicit economy, and, even more important, German Auto Salvage taught me about professionalism, auto mechanics, and maintaining a steady job. I stayed at German Auto for over a year until I found a better paying job as an expediter, later a busboy, and then a waiter at a local steak house called Charlie Brown's. These strong connections with mentors and the solid work opportunities they helped me obtain offered me a viable choice, and I never returned to the streets to steal or to sell drugs. In fact, for the next decade, I worked at least twenty hours a week, while continuing my education.

Despite drifting in and out of street life and hanging out with my homeboys for a few more years, I found I was able to exist in two worlds: fixing people's cars or serving food with courtesy and professionalism, on one hand, and engaging in turf disputes and putting myself at risk of arrest and victimization, on the other. By age seventeen, I had returned to school with a serious outlook and was shifting seamlessly between these various settings—school, probation, the street gang, the workplace—adopting a different persona for each. At school, I was the street kid turned legit; with my probation officer, I was the reformed criminal; on the street, I was that homie who had put in work, but now was less willing to break the law because of the greater risk of going to prison; at work, I was the fast-learning, hardworking kid eager for promotions who dreamed of going to college.

But without opportunities as a fifteen-year-old youth, flat on my ass amid a hail of shotgun fire, desperate for money and a place on the street, I could have easily remained like many of my peers—a human target. To be a human target is to be victimized and considered an enemy by others; it is to be viewed as a threat by law enforcement and schools and to be treated with stigma, disrepute, and punishment. Elsewhere, I have written that mass incarceration and punitive social control have constructed the treatment of a generation of marginalized youths as perennial criminals in need of control and containment, before they even commit their first offense; they encounter what I have termed "the youth control complex" (Rios 2011). Not all marginalized young people are as fortunate. In my professional career, as I have worked with young people who were labeled as deviant or criminal, I have found the dominant approach to reform these youngsters is to crack down on them, punish them until they follow directions, or harass and brutalize them to teach them a lesson. What allowed me to eventually turn conventional and escape being a perpetual target was not just an ability to code switch among my environments—something many urban youths learn on the streets—but also encountering tangible resources that caring adults facilitated for me: connections to meaningful educational, social, and labor market opportunities; the knowledge to recognize opportunity and take advantage of it; and the support to fortify my education-oriented aspirations, expectations, and day-to-day behaviors (see Vigil 1988).

In *Punished: Policing the Lives of Black and Latino Boys* (2011), I wrote about how some young people in the inner city grow up policed and punitively controlled by schools, parents, law enforcement, and others. I demonstrated how punishment operates as a social fabric of everyday life for marginalized young men. These young people experienced a kind of social death; they were outcasts before they even committed their first offense. This kind of targeting creates a system that metes out brutal symbolic and physical force on young people. In essence, young people become targets for police, schools, and other systems of social control to aim punitive resources and treatment at. This study lays out the interactional dynamics that take place within these punitive contexts, within a culture obsessed with control.[2]

In this book, I offer an analysis of the quality of interactions between authority figures and youths and of how these interactions impact the ways these youths engage with institutional actors; of how they view themselves, their social contexts, their futures; and of how they behave. I analyze how culture plays a key role in determining the well-being of young people that navigate punitive institutional settings. I show how, in attempting to support or reform youths placed at risk, schools and police develop practices that contradict good intentions.[3] These actions support a specific kind of cultural framing in young people that often leads them to further criminalization. In the end, I argue that institutional process and power overdetermine young people's ability to adopt and refine specific cultural practices and actions that impact their well-being. I also include recommendations for program and policy solutions to the misunderstanding, misjudging, and mistreatment leveled on these youths that perpetuate their social misery.

Although the problem of hypercriminalization, targeting, and negative framing of marginalized youths of color is a massive issue, solutions are not impossible. For instance, when I demonstrated an interest in returning to school and finding a job, my teacher, probation officer, and potential employer responded with empathy and compassion. They provided resources, opportunities, and second chances that created a trajectory of social mobility for me. But few of the young people I shadowed encountered these kinds of empathy or resources. The many youths I have followed who did not graduate from high school or achieve social mobility encountered a lack of opportunities and resources to develop the skills, not just to survive, but to thrive. *SURVIVING V. THRIVING FRAMEWORK*

A "surviving" frame is one that allows young people to utilize the street-life skills that they have learned to persist in a world with few social and material resources. A "thriving" frame is one that influences young people to seek out the skills to accomplish conventional goals, like acquiring a job, doing well in school, and desisting from health-compromising behaviors. As I developed a "thriving" frame for becoming an adult, mentors taught me to recognize and utilize these opportunities. Finally, the opportunities that I was given were culturally relevant, resonated with my tastes, desires, and aspirations, pulling me away from street life into a more conventional livelihood. As I moved beyond surviving to thriving, I remember telling myself when temptations arose to return to crime: "Don't just do what you *gotta* do; do what you *have* to do." I was reminding myself to utilize productive strategies for dealing with conflict, stress, and adversity. My sense of responsibility changed because I found a viable support system to enhance and promote a more positive, productive persona.

Multiple Identities, Multiple Settings

Over the years, I have questioned what prompted me to shift drastically between a harmful street life and informal economy, the conventional labor market, and eventually back to school. In many ways, this was the motivation for this study. Was this kaleidoscope of multiple identities displayed within one day's time unique to my life? Could other young people, caught up in the juvenile justice system and street life, also drift between different identities, and if so, under what conditions would each performance dominate?[4] What might be the implications for programs and policies if we were to recognize that young people indeed have the ability to shift seamlessly between conventional and deviant displays with minimal intervention and within a few hours' time? What role could institutions play in providing young people with the resources for shifting between these presentations of self?

The research on juvenile delinquents that I have encountered seems to contradict my personal experience and that of the young people I have shadowed over the course of ten years. The literature typically depicts various dichotomous typologies—the street kid, the decent kid, the clean kid, the dirty kid—that are seemingly fixed with one master identity. But in the real world, there is no such thing as fixed types. The angry person is only angry for a set amount of time; after, we might find that he is sad, happy, excited, et cetera.[5] Identities also shift on a consistent basis. For example, consider the multiple identities that college students navigate. They can simultaneously be one or more of the following: young adults, athletes, obnoxious drunks, travelers, cheaters, daughters, boyfriends, drug users, deviants, assholes, and social justice champions.

Some of the street-life-oriented young people I have studied do present aggressive tendencies, at times. However, more common are young people who shift their practices, actions, and attitudes across short time spans (e.g., a few hours) and spaces (e.g., between school and the street). They may be persistently vulnerable, but they are hardly static in the ways in which they navigate their worlds. I have discovered that youths can consistently adopt different personae, and *institutions play an integral role in the types of performances these youths enact and the sorts of cultural frames they engage* (see Vigil 1988; Harding 2010; Conchas and Vigil 2012). Instead of thinking of people as fixed types, we should view them as actors dynamically responding on a stage with constantly shifting backdrop and scenery, their performances influenced by different settings and different actors they encounter. This process is difficult to analyze because in the real time in vivo world, the individuals we study continually and consistently shape-shift. Since we are trying to capture patterns and replicable understandings, we tend to write about people in one-dimensional, practicable ways. Researchers in many ways are like still photography cameras. We collect a plethora of images that represent the real world but these images can only portray specific, frozen in time moments. We should strive to be more like video cameras in that we represent the multiple dimensions that we encounter in the real world. Following young people across institutional settings allows us to see these multidimensions and the many impediments and supports various institutions provide.[6]

In order to understand how this process of shifting personae operates among marginalized young people, I decided to shadow those considered a high threat in the community they lived in— gang members. Most books about gangs focus on the life stories, group processes, perspectives, structural impediments, criminal behaviors, life outcomes, or resistance strategies of gang members (see, e.g., Vigil 2002). Although such interrogations provide valuable

Handwritten margin notes: Resistance to have multiple forms of navig-

insights, this book takes a different tack to focus on the outcomes of interactions between gang-associated youths and the institutional actors they encounter. I utilize the phrase "gang-associated" to describe individuals who have been labeled or self-describe as gang members (typically, the former is more common). "Associated" helps to remind us that many gang members are actually gang members because they have been labeled as such. A "gang" is just that, a label. When we forget this caveat, we perpetuate ideas of inner-city youths as violent criminals—an identity often connected to gang member in conventional discourse. To understand the multiple dimensions of these young people that are typically seen as one-dimensional gangsters, I shadow them from multiple angles.

Let's imagine that a helmet camera has been attached to the youths you will meet in this book, and what you see are snippets of youths' experiences as they navigate multiple settings. This narrative view emerges from interviews, focus groups, and observations. In addition, let's imagine the camera capturing these youths' lives has a zoom-out lens so you can see the youths themselves, the institutional actors they encounter, and the settings they navigate. Let's also imagine that another camera is recording from across the room or across the street, providing a vantage point from which I can make observations about the youths and their interactions with institutional actors. In this way, I have applied a triangulated method in which interviews, observations, and focus groups yield insights from various viewpoints in the field.[7] Readers who wish to learn more about this triangulated method and my "shadowing" approach may read the methodological appendix.

I am not interested in creating yet another sensationalistic or celebratory book about "ghetto denizens" or "gangbangers," but rather in providing a deeper understanding of the processes by which authority figures fail to support young people and to recognize their multiple dimensions and multiple selves and how young people fail to demonstrate to the system their readiness to change. I show that as police and educators—often with good intention—try to reform or support young people, they create human targets: youths produced and portrayed as risks and criminal threats. As a result, they deliver punitive treatment at these youth, expecting a positive response. Instead of reforming, young people recognize this systematic targeting and look for ways to get the bull's-eye off their backs or to fight back. This targeting leads young people to drift between conventional and self-compromising identities, while authority figures also vacillate between restorative and punitive social control in dealing with these disreputable individuals.

Pernicious Fire

CULTURE OF CNTRL

Criminologist David Garland has argued that the United States has developed a culture of control. This culture of control is characterized by a deep-seated fear of crime; marginalized, primarily poor, populations rendered as criminal threats; the expansion of punitive legal sanctions; the obsessive focus on victims; and the manipulation of crime issues for political gain. Culture becomes a powerful, lone-standing vessel that helps to produce social marginalization through punitive mechanisms (Garland 2001b). But what does this culture of control look like in real time? How does it come to affect the lives of those individuals that become its targets? The aim of this book is to provide an ethnographic archaeology of the processes that this culture of control imposes on marginalized youths, and the cultural formations that circumscribe these young people's lives as they engage with punitive structures.

As human targets, young people inevitably encounter pernicious fire—the meting out on individuals any number of detrimental outcomes, such as institutional stigmatization, school suspensions or expulsions, police harassment and humiliation, or disproportionate arrest and incarceration. Pernicious fire can evoke a life of social misery—like when an individual is pushed out of school or granted a criminal record and is unable to find viable employment. The more that authority figures misunderstand and mistreat marginalized populations, the more likely they are to resort to pernicious fire. This notion of pernicious fire is both a metaphor for the continuum of

"trough on crime" "trough immig. laws"

I think that is precisely why representation matters.

punitive treatment across institutional settings and an observation of the trajectory of social action that leads to lethal outcomes, like police killings of unarmed males of color.

In recent years in the United States, a spree of police shootings of unarmed young men of color has made national news. In 2016, Alton Sterling, a black male in Louisiana, and Pedro Villanueva, a Latino male in California, were both shot and killed by police. Both of them were unarmed. While Sterling's case made national headlines, Villanueva's killing did not receive much national media attention. It appears that when Latinos are killed by police, the national media does not pay as much attention to the issue, diminishing the story of the punitive and violent policing of Latinos in the United States. But, as I demonstrate in this book, poor Latino youths encounter punitive and violent police treatment that is also worthy of national attention.

Police killings of unarmed men of color have also spurred some of the most vibrant, massive, controversial, and prolific social movements among marginalized classes in recent history. Two more of many cases were the killings of Michael Brown and Andy Lopez. Michael Brown, an unarmed, black eighteen-year-old, was fatally shot by a white police officer on August 9, 2014, in the Saint Louis suburb of Ferguson, Missouri. Brown's murder sparked near immediate protests in Ferguson as well as national media attention as residents called for an end to the pattern of police assaults on members of the black majority in a city with predominately white government officials (Bouie 2014; Schuman 2014). Andy Lopez, a thirteen-year-old Latino resident of Santa Rosa, California, was shot and killed by a white sheriff's deputy when the officer mistook Lopez's airsoft gun—a nonlethal replica of an AK-47—for an actual firearm. Similar to the Brown incident, protests were organized in Santa Rosa and throughout California to draw attention to an epidemic of police brutality (Alexander 2013). These young men represent just two examples in the national crisis of police misreading, misunderstanding, misjudging, and dehumanizing young males of color.

When police officers don't understand and fear the bodies, culture, and actions of young black and Latino men—when they mis-recognize and misframe them—they can make reckless decisions that invite unjust treatment, violence, and even death. Police operate in a larger cultural context in which they are socialized and taught to fear males of color. From a very young age, some youths are constructed as human targets by this culture of control, and when they encounter police mistreatment and violence, many in society may have come to believe these young people deserve such targeting and even eradication, leading to a culture of impunity within law enforcement departments across the nation. When police are trained by their departments to shoot when they feel that their life is in jeopardy, these fears, combined with the a system of impunity that does not hold officers accountable for unjustified killings, can play a major role in the split-second decision to shoot and kill a black or Latino male. Within this culture of control, officers are implicitly taught and allowed to operate under the assumption that blacks and Latinos are a threat and that their lives don't matter. While most police stops do not end in a killing, many police stops do result in negative interactions. It is these micro-punitive processes that build up over time, leading to negative community-police relations, resentments toward police, and racist policing.

Ultimately, I seek to demonstrate in this book how our punitive attempts to help, regulate, and control disreputable youths can end up creating a larger crisis of control and can lead to school failure and police violence. The unfortunate outcomes are entire communities that are hyperpoliced and hyperincarcerated (see Rios 2011; Fader 2013; Goffman 2014), tens of thousands of dollars spent to imprison even one person each year (California spends $47,421 in tax dollars per prisoner annually),[8] and the perpetuation and accentuation of the social misery that poverty already brings to these young people. This crisis of control plays out through culture: day-to-day practices, negative interactions, and contested symbols that come to frame young people's understanding of their social world.

If we want heroin-selling, gangbanging, car-thieving, juvenile delinquents to reform and work toward developing productive lives, then institutions, especially schools and law enforcement, must find ways to improve the quality of their interactions with these youths, provide them with meaningful resources to thrive on, and celebrate and promote their innate ability to shift between a myriad of identities and personas. We must develop programs and policies that account for the multiple scenes and backdrops that these youths regularly encounter as they seamlessly shift with fluidity through various daily settings. The culture of control must be replaced with a culture of care; we must stop setting young people up as targets and instead treat them as seeds to be nurtured.

CULTURE OF CARE

Study Participants and Setting

I observed the institutional and personal stories of gang-associated young people in a Southern California community I have renamed "Riverland." In order to protect the confidentiality of the participants in this study, I have created pseudonyms for them, their community, and the city they are from. While descriptions and news reports might expose the location and identity of some of the participants in this study, I have done my best to report findings that minimize vulnerability that this study might place them in.

Many youths that I initially encountered had multiple stories of racism, humiliation, and punishment meted out by schools and police; I wanted to explore firsthand what they experienced as human targets. I sought to collect information from multiple angles to unearth the logic and practice of this targeting process, of this culture of control. I conducted five years of observations, from 2007 to 2012, and interviews on street corners and in parks, a community center, courtrooms, a probation school, and a conventional high school. The study began at Punta Vista, a school for youths on probation, where I eventually conducted two years of observations. At that school, I developed relationships with some youths from the south side, who facilitated my encounters with other out-of-school, gang-associated youths.

Throughout the study, I observed and interviewed fifty-seven

57 latino (15-22)
boys/men

18 girls

Latino gang-associated males between fifteen and twenty-one years old in various settings; interviewed and observed eighteen gang-associated females, primarily at Punta Vista School; and supervised fourteen focus groups with females and forty-two with males. In this particular community, gang-associated females had a less visible presence, and as a male researcher, I felt a limited ability to gain trust and shadow the young women I encountered. Latina women experience a very unique trajectory from that of Latino men in the criminal justice system (see Diaz-Coto 2006). In addition, my research objective was to try to understand a group that is disproportionately represented as human targets, bearing the brunt of harsh school discipline, arrest, and incarceration—young males of color. Therefore, I chose to focus primarily on male gang-associated youths, while drawing insights from the young women whom I managed to interview and informally observe.[9]

Over the years, a team of eight graduate students and fourteen undergraduate students helped me to conduct focus groups and interviews for this study. Their research was primarily conducted at the local community center where we met with gang-associated youths as a team once a week on Friday evenings over the course of four years and where I could supervise them as they helped to collect interview and focus group data. Although I organized a research team to help with this project, I alone collected the systematic observational data outside of the community center in order to maintain consistency and to avoid exposing students to risk. While some of my students went on to conduct observations for their own independent research projects, the fieldwork observations that I report on in this book are my own, unless otherwise reported with "we" instead of "I." Chapter 3 was coauthored with Patrick Lopez-Aguado, chapter 4 was coauthored with Rachel Sarabia, and chapter 5 was coauthored with Samuel Gregory Prieto—all graduate students under my supervision at the time. They helped to collect and analyze data and to provide me with insight on my coding, theoretical memos, and preliminary conclusions, in order to ensure that at least one other person was seeing the patterns I uncovered in the field.

Setting and Study

Riverland is a Southern California city known as an idyllic beach-side community. Its beautiful coastal geography inflates real estate values, attracting development of hidden mansions along hillsides that offer scenic ocean views, as well as upscale boutiques along Beach Street, the main corridor for the downtown commercial district. Home to numerous theaters, museums, and vacation homes, the city sells itself as having the culture and sophistication of California's larger elite cities without the big-city problems of crime or poverty. Through the prioritizing and policing of public space, Riverland works hard to maintain the popular perception that it is exclusively wealthy and white.

But despite its tranquil image, Riverland is not immune from race and class conflicts. A few blocks from Beach Street, Chavez Avenue cuts through South Riverland as a kind of second main street, one that caters to the city's overlooked Latino population. Largely hidden from Riverland's projected image and rarely acknowledged in positive reporting by local media, Latinos comprise approximately 30 percent of the city's population, and most of these residents work in the low-wage service sector. South Riverland houses many residents of color, positioned as a servant class to the larger population, who struggle to survive in face of the extravagant cost of living, one of the nation's highest. Some of them live in dire conditions and express a desire for better living conditions. Thirty-one-year-old Cristina, mother of Rosy, a fourteen-year-old gang-associated girl, explained:

> I would like them to have the basic resources they need. How do I
> help them, if I don't have the money? . . . Rosy doesn't get a good
> lunch. She comes home hungry, and I don't have much. I want to be
> able to provide them with the basics: shoes, food. I want to be able
> to feed my kids, to clothe them. I think that has a lot to do with how
> she acts. She gets frustrated with our situation. Frustrated over not
> having anything and living the life we live. I think this lifestyle is

what drives her to hang out with her friends in the street; drives her to stay on the streets with her sister rather than come home. They have food. She is probably tired of Top Ramen or Cup-o-Noodles, or canned vegetables or peas, but that is what I can afford and sometimes they are free from the church. We don't even have money for laundry detergent. We have been wearing dirty clothes for the last few days. We haven't washed in three weeks.

The youths in this community commonly find themselves publicly racially profiled as criminal others. The local division of labor that designates Latinos as low-end service workers who cater to wealthy residents and tourists reinforces racial tensions.[10] These status differences, which are most visible at school and in encounters with whites, remind youths of color that they are considered "dangerous, fearsome" people, a designation that is ironically both stigmatizing and empowering. The youths' responses are varied, but some turn to gang culture and life, like Rosy. Youths who adopt gang-associated attire find they have the power to cause a reaction—usually a negative one, within a context in which they are feared. Johny, a sixteen-year-old gang-involved Latino, explained:

If you go with your homies, they stare at you. Baggy clothes make you look suspicious . . . around here if you're walking in a little group. People are all scared of you. . . . If *gueros* [whites] are coming toward you, they'll get off the sidewalk so you can pass by. They're scared as fuck!

Latino youths report other encounters with white residents that serve to reinforce the local economic hierarchies. Johny continued:

I used to work at the farmers' market with my father, and there was white people that would give you attitude about the color skin that you are. 'Cause I'm working behind this table selling these things to you don't mean you have to be rude to me, 'cause you don't have to buy them from me and feel like I need you.[11]

Race and class become inextricably tangled as young Latinos are expected to represent a working class that serves the wealthier white
locals. But rather than submit to class oppression and become "good
workers" while being robbed of opportunities to obtain viable occu-
pations, these youths become defiant against the exploitive status
thrust upon them.[1] Within a culture of control, these young people
have come to be feared and constructed as criminal threats rather
than docile, exploitable, "well-behaved" workers.

may this be a generational trend?

In Riverland, race and class marginalization also occurs in
schools. Sixteen-year-old Mary, a student who was expelled for fighting and sent to the probation school, Punta Vista, shared her perspective:

> I think they feel that like white kids are like better . . . like Mexican
> kids are, I guess, like gang-related and I think they think they're like
> bad influences, and they think we're like not smart. They think that
> like white kids are . . . smart, and they're like good kids, they're like
> good influences. . . . You could tell how the teachers are like how they
> look at you before you even start dressing different.[13]

This criminal labeling becomes a self-fulfilling prophecy for
many youths of color. Another gang-associated male, sixteen-year-
old Tito, experienced similar treatment and pinpointed an incident
that strongly influenced his decision to adopt a "gang" style and drop
out of school: "'The teacher chose . . . me, and the white guy [a fellow
student],' he said, 'Oh, he won't know the answer. He's Mexican.' The
teacher didn't say anything."

When I asked him how he felt about this, he said,

> I felt like shit, so I just skip school. Go to a friend's house, help my
> parents with work, do drugs, fucking just go look for fights, go to
> Beach Street. Just anything rather than school. I hate school.

For many of these youths, school becomes a place where they feel
disrespected and reprimanded rather than educated, and as a re-

sult, they develop an oppositional stance toward educational institutions and seek alternative spaces for acceptance and affirmation (Dance 2002). One such surrogate is the street and gang life. Once associated with this world, young people find it more difficult to succeed in school and the labor market, and they get caught up in the criminal justice system. Institutional labels and the way in which institutions treat these gang-associated youths play a role in young people's well-being.

→ School to prison pipeline .

What's in a Label?

After gathering data in the field for a year, I developed a conceptual and theoretical framework in order to understand the processes by which labeling shaped the kinds of cultural and material resources, and by default life outcomes, that marginalized Latino youths encountered. This section describes the conceptual and theoretical framework I utilize and develop. Readers who wish to immediately learn more about the youths in this study, their contexts, and their stories may skip to chapter 1.

To be "from the south side" carried multiple meanings in Riverland. One could have grown up there, resided in a south side neighborhood, or be formally labeled as a member of the south side gang by schools or law enforcement. This ambiguous labeling created immense problems for law enforcement, schools, and the media as they sought to determine who was a gang member and who was not. Often, these parties—along with social scientists—have been content with a loose definition of a gang member that could be applied to youths who wear symbols, enact mannerisms, hang out in specific areas, and represent specific racialized populations. Entire books on "gangs" have been written by social scientists without clearly defining how they determined gang membership. Decker and Van Winkle's *Life in the Gang* (1996) is one example. In describing gang activity and behavior, these authors make it appear as if all the youths in the community they studied were gang members. The uncritical assumption that these and other "gang experts" make is that living in poverty, being of color, and having a tight-knit group of friends renders one a gang member and, therefore, an ideal research subject.[14] Gang researchers must reflect on the process by which they determine gang membership, and find strategies for determining if their definitions hold any value in the real world, prior to conducting their studies. Otherwise, they risk misrepresenting the lives of marginalized youths and influencing practice and policy based on fallacy.

For this research, I sought to bypass simplistic, racist labels devoid of empirical evidence that are frequently applied to urban youths of color. Instead, I refer to the boys in this study as "gang-associated." To be gang-associated is to be perceived as, self-reported as, or informally or formally labeled (typically by law enforcement or schools) as an actual gang member. The reason I utilize this label is to address the ambiguity that exists in the study of gangs. "Associated" here refers to those cognitive, institutional, or interactional processes by which individuals are connected to the gang life. This line of reasoning helps us acknowledge that the research and writing we conduct is also embedded within a larger culture of control that influences the intersubjective construction of reality that our work produces. In other words, researchers can be just as complicit in constructing marginalized populations as criminal threats in need of regulation and control.

How do we know who is a gang member? Sometimes, when young people self-report, they have their own arbitrary definitions of what a gang is. Some believe a crew of three friends with a moniker for their group is a gang; others believe that you are not a gang member until you have been officially initiated by a street gang under the jurisdiction of a recognized prison gang, such as the Mexican Mafia or *Nuestra Familia*. In one instance, police formally entered a fourteen-year-old in a statewide gang database—CalGang, hosted and supported by the California Department of Justice—simply because he wore a hat bearing his childhood nickname, *Flaco* (Skinny), on the bottom flap. Was he a gang member? Other times, without any justification other than their biased judgment or a few disciplinary incidents, or the youth's tough demeanor, school officials have been convinced that a kid is a gang member. The youth is labeled and treated accordingly: zero-tolerance dress codes, assignment to special programs, and interactions based on disdain, pity, or fear.

The gang label is a powerful one that generates specific resources, actions, and interactions within the various institutions these young people must navigate.[15] For example, during my time in the field, researchers at the University of California, Santa Barbara, had helped to create a "risk assessment" instrument for the county probation department to survey probation youths about their attitudes toward violence and crime. The youths were also asked whether their relatives where gang involved or in jail or prison. The intent was to collect data on the resources that these young people needed to facilitate their reform. During four court observations, I witnessed prosecutors using these instruments to make a case against some of the boys.[16] The logic: If the young man reported that his older brother was in jail and in a gang, then he was at risk of committing a crime as well and, therefore, should be given a harsher sentence to prevent that crime from occurring.[17]

According to criminologist and former gang member Robert Durán (2013), gang membership is socially constructed, and "there is nothing [finite] that establishes when people join or leave." Therefore, it is difficult to determine who is a gang member and when the person joins or leaves the gang. Research has shown that "most people fade away from the gang scene" (Durán 2013, 24) as they mature. But despite the fact that most gang members have been found to disengage from gang activity within two to three years from initiation, the effects of the gang label last much longer. When law enforcement or schools label a young person as a gang member, that youth is likely to face grave consequences independent of any possible criminal activity he may engage in, past, present, or future. These consequences might include indefinite registry in the gang databases, automatic gang enhancements if convicted of a future crime, stigma and negative treatment from authority figures, and injunctions prohibiting being physically present in certain loca-

tions, including educational facilities such as high schools and community colleges. In this study, I found that gang labeling resulted
in stigma, exclusion, and subsequent arrests, even years after the
youngsters had left the street life.[18]

Based on the findings in this study and insight from Brotherton
and Barrios's (2004) gang definition, I developed a working definition for the gang: a group process that occurs as marginalized young
people attempt to provide each other, within a collective context, a
dignified identity, "an opportunity to feel individually and collectively empowered, a voice to speak back to, challenge," and engage
the dominant culture and institutions of social control, "a refuge
from the stresses and strains of poverty," and a protective factor—a
surrogate—that functionally and perceivably replaces the role that
institutions of socialization and support (schools, the family, the
welfare system) have failed to provide. In essence, a gang, and a gang
member, are not a what but a how (Vigil 2002). They are not things
or people; they are processes. In the United States, the gang label is
heavily racialized. In the media and with law enforcement, a group
of Latino or black youths committing a crime is likely to be labeled
as a gang. This is not the case with groups of white youths who commit similar crime (Covington 2010).

Because a gang is socially constructed, its definition must be fluid
enough to allow for local context, nuanced group processes, and the
autonomous power of labeling. By extension, if an institution defines a group of disreputable youths as a gang, then regardless of any
specific characteristics or function, that group is, in effect, a gang.
Institutional power defines who is a gang member and what constitutes a gang threat. Once defined, we must account for the racialized
response to this perceived gang threat, the quality of interactions
between the gang and authority figures, the group and cultural processes that ensue from this label, and the reactions provoked. To
understand young people who have been labeled as gang members,
we must observe them in various facets of their lives, at different
times and space points, and across different settings. We must also

understand their multiple selves. A cultural framing perspective helps in this endeavor.

Cultural Framing

Cultural framing offers an analytical tool for understanding the role that institutions play in influencing young peoples' worldviews and actions. A cultural frame is a system of meaning-making, identity formation, and presentation of self based on material and symbolic resources that influence peoples' perceptions of the world and of their choice of actions and behaviors. Sociologist Ann Swidler (1986) describes this system as a cultural "toolkit" that individuals use to develop "strategies of action" (273).[19] Cultural frames influence how individuals think about their social and personal mobility and "how they choose to act" (Young 2004, 11). All populations in society draw upon a variety of cultural models, often coexisting simultaneously, to inform their actions. An array of cultural frames comprises an individual's understanding of the world and this "system of meaning" serves as the basis for future behavior (Geertz 1973). Likewise, individuals living in poverty are not bound by a fixed value system, but are surrounded by multiple cultural frames—what David Harding (2010) refers to as "cultural heterogeneity"—that offer various models for shaping perceptions, worldviews, and actions.[20] Social psychology research offers a similar conception—shape shifting— the intricate process of identity change (see Burke and Stets 2009; Alvermann et. al. 2006).

Culture provides resources from which individuals can draw to shape the outcomes of their actions, and structural opportunities determine which resources individuals will utilize in the various contexts they navigate. So when a young person has a negative interaction with an authority figure who represents a specific institution, the frames that inform the young person's actions are limited to a minimal selection of responses, often either to resist or reject the system, to develop what sociologist L. Janelle Dance calls "tough fronts" (2005). A healthy selection of responses might include asking for a meeting to address the issue, writing a letter to the school district, or having parents or lawyers intervene (assuming that these actions will be taken seriously by the system). However, these responses are limited by class or by the school's unwillingness to allow for these kinds of kids to respond in these kinds of ways. In this way, institutions play a key role in the process by which individuals encounter and utilize cultural frames. Schools and law enforcement can either help young people resonate with productive frames or hinder their connection with these frames.

Cultural frames structure how we interpret events and how we react to them, though the relationship between culture and behavior is not "cause-and-effect," but rather "a relationship that highlights constraint-and-possibility" (Small 2004). Although the youths in this study were influenced by cultural frames in near proximity—for example, gangsterism, defiance, and criminality—these frames did not cause their actions, but only made certain kinds of behavior more recognizable, accessible, and likely.

A cultural frames approach offers a more nuanced way to view young people's behaviors and reactions than the "typologies" model—the angry kid, the gang member, the decent type, dirty people, clean people—which assigns labels to individuals based on recurring observed attributes or based on labels imposed by others in the community. This approach renders individuals incapable of acting any other way. With a cultural frames approach, or what I refer to as an "Urban Dynamism" approach, we allow ourselves the capability to observe individuals change their dispositions and behaviors based on their encounters with power (in this case institutions) and as they cross institutional settings. David Harding (2010) provides a compelling theoretical model for understanding inner-city youths through a cultural framing perspective. This model has the potential to move urban ethnography, criminology, and other research on poor populations beyond typologizing approaches that caricaturize and at times even pathologize the populations we study.[21]

Harding argues that young people living in poverty have access to conventional cultural models, such as acquiring a college education or becoming responsible parents, and, indeed, aspire to achieve these goals; however, with limited resources to reach their aspirations, they inevitably follow other stronger models that resonate the most with their lived experience. Thus, cultural heterogeneity takes a different form in low-income settings based on the neighborhood context. Take, for example, the youngster in a poor neighborhood who aspires to go to college. His single mother may constantly push him to achieve his goal, but his peers on the streets and older siblings may support an alternative, survival-based frame: make some money to make ends meet. From their viewpoint, the strongest indicator of success may mean evading arrest or living another day without being victimized. Although an educational credential may be a highly valued aspiration, the immediate neighborhood context makes it a far-fetched idea and a less valuable indicator of success for these young people. As sixteen-year-old Mario phrased it, "A piece of paper [high school diploma] ain't gonna work as a bulletproof vest or stop the *puercos* [pigs] from violating me [arrest for violating terms of probation]."

Cultural heterogeneity exists in all social environments among all social groups; however, poor neighborhoods lack resources to support certain specific cultural frames. Therefore, the more positive aspiration (going to college) can be diluted and less influential, while the negative, more immediate goal (surviving violence, staying out of trouble) can be amplified. This process, which Harding calls "model shifting," occurs when young people adopt the salient frames for their neighborhood context.

Harding's study focused on the influence of neighborhoods and peers, but did not analyze the role authority figures and institutional powers play in shaping the cultural models that influence young people's understandings and actions. In this study of Riverland youths, I examine how young people's model shifting unfolds across institutional settings—the probation school, the streets, the community center, the conventional high school, and the legal system—and the role that institutional actors play in how young people interpret and utilize cultural frames. In other words, institutional processes have a profound influence on the cultural models available to youths and the cultural models that young people choose to engage with. For example, Mark, a fifteen-year-old gang-associated student, wanted to go to college, and he even demonstrated that he knew the steps needed to obtain a four-year college degree, as in this conversation with me:

> v.r.: Do you know the steps needed to get to college, to get a degree?
>
> MARK: Get some, like two years of CC [community college] classes and get good grades. Then I apply to transfer to get a business degree.
>
> v.r.: What prevents you from taking these steps, what obstacles do you face?
>
> MARK: A bunch of lame-ass shit. Like my record and my grades and my attitude and these dumb-ass probation officers and teachers that don't get me.... Every day, I guess, it's like I just have to avoid getting caught up, staying legit.
>
> v.r.: You sound like you know what it takes to stay legit. Why do you think you still get caught up even though you know how to avoid it?
>
> MARK: You can leave the streets, but the streets aren't gonna leave you. At the end of the day that's all you got. Your homies there waiting, backing you up, needing a favor . . . but the school side what does it have to offer you?

To Mark, planning for college represented a relevant, albeit muted, system of ideas and practices that signaled his desire to extend his education and someday become a professional. Another positive frame was "staying legit," which meant avoiding academic failure, victimization, incarceration, and acquiring resources through legitimate economic and financial means. Youths like Mark could be drawn to these positive frames, but authority figures' either subtle or overt countermessages may result in them turning back to the street—a landscape with a stronghold on the boys' decision making.

Indeed, as I examined the quality of interactions between youths and authority figures, I uncovered how cultural heterogeneity functions across institutional settings and how it's impacted by institutional power. To deal with youths' disreputable behaviors, police and school officials attempted to incorporate young people's alternative "street" frames into the informal rules and interactions they propagated. As a result, good or neutral intentions often constructed negative outcomes.

Negative interactions can determine worldviews and outcomes for marginalized young people. Authority figure–youth interactions were dominated by misrecognition: the process by which an individual fails in understanding the meaning and intentions attached to the cultural framing that the other is engaged in. When students' actions were misinterpreted, they responded with resistance.[22] Resistance became cognition: Young people became aware of the crisis of control and institutional failure to regulate their behavior and, in turn, consciously attempted to persist and generate alternative protective factors. A failure of control at school and other institutions produced collective identities, frames of resistance, and protective mechanisms among these marginalized youths. This, in turn, fueled the culture of control, resulting in harsher interactions and punishments. The quality of interactions between youths and authorities had a tremendous impact on youths' attitudes and decisions, which, in turn, profoundly affected their lives as they neared adulthood. Schools and police, like the streets, limited the cultural models young people could realistically pursue, and those limitations shaped how they engaged with authority figures. I first observed these processes of cultural (mis)framing at the local probation school, Punta Vista, where my study began.

Punta Vista served as a revealing opening site for this research because the various forces I sought to study seemed to converge there: the culture of control, cultural heterogeneity, gang-associated youths, delinquent youths, high school dropouts (more sensible label: pushouts), probation officials, police, educators, and community and social services.

CHAPTER ONE

The Probation School

Punta Vista School opened its doors in the early 1990s in Riverland, California, as an alternative institution for educating students who were failing school or in trouble with the law. Juveniles on probation and students expelled from local high schools—usually for gang-related truancy, defiance, fights, and drug use—were mandated to attend Punta Vista School. Its mission was to educate those youths released from incarceration or those truants who had missed too many days at the conventional school to be allowed to return.

Jorge and Mark were two of the first youths I met at Punta Vista. Over time, I shadowed and interviewed them to learn about the institutional forces that converged to impact them. Punta Vista School and the surrounding streets of South Riverland formed the main nexus where youths like Jorge and Mark interacted with authority figures. Eventually, I hung out on the streets of the south side and in other relevant places—the conventional high school, the community center, and the courtroom—to follow up with Jorge, Mark, and other gang-associated youths.

For two months, I observed classes at Punta Vista before I approached Mark and Jorge, gang-associated youths who had reported being previously arrested and listed in law enforcement's gang database. They were also described by school officials as gang members. Over the years, the boys shifted between labeling themselves as gang members or alleged gang members, depending on their attitudes and circumstances. The boys agreed to allow me to interview and observe them. In addition, Jorge and Mark connected me with other gang-associated young men in the neighborhood. With this snowball method, I gained access to members of a male street gang that law enforcement had linked with the Mexican Mafia, a notorious prison gang that was otherwise suspicious of outsiders.[1]

Despite these introductions and connections, gaining the trust of some of these young men was not easy. In fact, some stated that they did not trust me even after four years in the field. Their main concern was that one day I would turn data I collected over to law enforcement. Therefore, for the youths' safety and my own protection, over time I acquired a certificate of confidentiality from the U.S. Department of Health and Human Services, which allows the researcher to refuse to disclose identifiable research information in response to legal demands. Part of the certificate mandates that "persons so authorized to protect the privacy of such individuals may not be compelled in any Federal, State, or local civil, criminal, administrative, legislative, or other proceedings to identify such individuals." Eventually, some of the boys trusted me enough to allow me to shadow them at the park, the street, the community center, their schools, and at Golden State Liquors store.

When I first met Jorge, a short, scrawny fifteen-year-old Latino, he had a shaved head and preferred to dress in extra-baggy polyester work pants or shorts—Dickies or Ben Davis—and extra-large white T-shirts or blue-checkered dress shirts. He was in fourth grade when he and his older brother arrived undocumented to the United States from Mexico, and he still spoke with a heavy accent, struggling to find words in English as quickly as he wanted to say them. He often switched back and forth between English and Spanish: "*Ay ese cabron is talking shit about me; si no se calla le voy a dar en la madre*" [Ay, that asshole is talking shit about me; if he doesn't shut up I am going to kick his ass]. Jorge's response to his environment and the stress inflicted on him was to make jokes and witty comments. From his seat at the front of the class, he cracked jokes, chatted with classmates, blurted out random noises, and constantly frustrated the teacher with back talk.

Mark was a *Californio* (Mexican and indigenous origin) whose family roots could be traced back to California native peoples and the Spanish who arrived in the seventeenth and eighteenth centuries, before the United States seized California from Mexico.[2] Mark was proud of his family's heritage ("My great grandma was Chumash [Native American], and all my family has been here way before the *gueros* [white people] came"), but he also used his deep roots with the land as a point of resistance to the Anglo culture's dominance, disrespect for indigenous and other cultures, and expectations of assimilation and submission to a given role in society.[3] Mark's experience illustrates Riverland's deeply problematic racialized culture in which Latinos are portrayed, described, and visible as either members of a servant class or a criminal class (see chapter 3). The servant class typically includes adult immigrants who work in the tourist and restaurant industries, while the criminal class comprises younger individuals, often second generation and beyond, who are constantly stopped and frisked by police in public and appear almost nightly on the evening news as criminal suspects or perpetrators. Mark, like many of the boys in this study, troubled with the community's treatment of his people, wanted to do something about the problem, but did not know how.

With his hair buzz-cut so short that his pale scalp was visible, Mark sat quietly at the back of the classroom, consistently appearing disgruntled. The administration and faculty had a list of character types, folk categories, used to label students for the sake of everyone's safety and to maintain order: the addict, the emotionally disturbed, the promiscuous *chola* (gangster girl), the angry *cholo*, the wannabe (aspiring gangster), and the class clown. The principal selected "the angry type" to describe Mark. He did appear to internalize his frustrations, and eventually he would reach a breaking point and lash out. One day, for example, Mark overheard a male classmate tell a female student, "I think you like Mark; I think you want him to ask you out?"

Mark's light complexion turned slightly red as he clinched his fists together and his face and the back of his head convulsed in anger. He stood up from his desk to confront the other boy: "What you say about me? Don't be putting my name in your stupid fucking words.... I'm gonna kick your ass after school!"

The classroom security guard, a typical fixture in a school for students considered at risk, swiftly grabbed Mark by the shoulder and marched him outside. Mark did not return for the remainder of class. Later, I noticed him sitting in the principal's office. "We have to give him lots of time to cool down," the security guard said.

Being removed from class was hardly new to Mark, whose disruptive behavior invited institutional reprimand from an early age. White boys displaying similar behavior in an affluent suburban school might be labeled ADHD (attention deficit/hyperactivity disorder), but, for Mark, the ritual was to be singled out and positioned as "gang" member.[4] Mark told me,

> Since like third grade I would like disrupt the class, according to them [teachers], I would always be disruptive. They would wait for me to say one little thing just to get me out of class . . . they wouldn't give me a chance . . . like then in high school my fuckin' English teacher, that fool, used to have my referrals already written for me—a big stack—he would wait just for me to say something and he'll be like all right go outside walk to the office . . . and I knew because they would always say the same, like no matter what I did, it would say "disruptive in class."

According to Mark, his disruptiveness led him to become labeled a gang member:

> I know like they don't want you there [at school], like gangsters like people that they think you know are gangsters. These motherfuckers, they're not doing, they're not gonna do any good to our school. Fuck that. Kick 'em out, you know try to find reasons to get 'em out. Like, oh yeah, this fool got suspended like three times, he's a gang member . . . that's what happened with me. Just for getting in trouble in class, they were scared and labeled me a fuckin' gangster and kicked me out.

During my observations, I found Mark had a tendency to respond to conflict through facial expressions and language that staff considered angry and threatening to others. Many times, I witnessed Mark become uncontrollably upset over an apparently trivial issue.[5] On one occasion, in front of the Golden State Liquors store, the preferred hangout spot for the south side boys, Mark loaned his brother, Justin, a pair of Locs sunglasses. Advertised as "the most popular hardcore shades in the world" and worn by famous rap artists like Ice Cube and the late Eazy-E, Locs sold for under twenty dollars and were coveted among the neighborhood boys.

(Justin, also one of the South Riverland gang-associated boys had been arrested for running away from a police officer who caught him breaking the 10 p.m. city curfew. The curfew bans youths under sixteen from being out without an adult chaperone at night, and violators are ticketed and ordered to appear in court to face financial penalties and possible probation. Justin attempted to flee before the ticket and the fine; instead, he was arrested and charged with violating the terms of his probation.[6])

That day in front of the liquor store, Justin accidently chipped Mark's Locs, which infuriated and enraged his brother. Mark started pacing and cursing, and then kicked the liquor store wall. Standing about three feet away from me, he slammed the sunglasses on the ground with all his might, shattering them into hundreds of tiny fragments. The loud noise followed by plastic shrapnel bouncing off my arms sent chills running through my body. The other boys looked shocked, and Mark walked away as if trying to stop himself from physically attacking his brother.

On the streets, such aggressive displays were prominent and threats or violent acts could unfold at any given moment. However, the Punta Vista School's authoritarian control kept such aggression to a minimum during the day and on site, saved for a later time and a different space. The school's primary role seemed to be to contain violent behavior in order to maintain a reputation of control. But what happened outside of school was out of its purview.

Despite his principal's description and my own initial observation of an ill-tempered Mark, he was more complicated than the "angry type" label suggested. I could have settled for studying Mark's dominant "angry" persona. Over the years, he demonstrated many episodes of rage and anger. However, I also realized that Mark had other ways of being, other identities, that the school had not recognized but that over time and across space, I could uncover.[7]

Observing young people across settings and for long periods of time allows us to uncover their multiple dimensions. It is our obligation as researchers to complicate our descriptions of these individuals so that our writing portrays a more true-to-life version of the individuals we encounter in the field. A more reflexive approach that understands research participants as heterogeneous in their worldviews and behaviors allows us to grant individuals the human dignity they deserve and to approach a more nuanced understanding of the social facts we examine.

Mark could have been understood in this project as simply an angry type, taking his frustration out on his peers and the system. However, Mark also portrayed other dominant characteristics that require further examination. For example, a few hours after the sunglasses incident, I observed Mark in front of his friend Michael's apartment talking to Michael's mother. He noticed that the front of her apartment smelled of urine and was filled with cigarette butts and trash. He said, "'*Spensa señora* [excuse me, ma'am], I can clean some of this stuff if you want. All I need is a bucket of water and a broom and a trash bag." Mark's relationship with this adult—an authority figure he respected and listened to—seemed to position him as a helper. In this different social context, Mark presented himself as kind and empathetic.

Among many youths in this study, I found a similar ability to switch personae and corresponding mannerisms from one social context to another. Labeled one way by authorities in a certain context, these same youths could present themselves as quite the opposite elsewhere. Some authority figures and some spatial and social contexts seemed to bring out the best in young people while others brought out the worst, and, more than distinct personalities, these interactional and spatial contexts mattered.

The Controlled Environment of Punta Vista

The interactional and spatial context of Punta Vista seemed to bring out the worst dimension in students. The school resembled an industrial building, about three thousand square feet and freshly painted institutional gray. The main door, painted green, seemed better suited to a residential house, hardly like a gateway through which dozens of high school students would walk each day. Three insignificant windows facing west brought minimal natural light into the school. Plumbing pipes, electrical wires, and utility meters covered about a fourth of the front facade. The parking lot had room for three cars, and a metal, barbed-wire fence, about eight-feet tall, divided the school from the adjacent sidewalk. A minuscule sign, two-inches wide by five-inches long, read "Punta Vista School." Local residents appeared clueless about this unattractive, seemingly vacant building.

Aside from the building's dreary appearance, the school site had been mired in controversy when toxic chemicals had seeped from abandoned, dilapidated underground oil and toxic waste storage tanks left behind from a diesel truck repair shop that once had been located on the adjacent property. In addition, the Department of Toxic Substances Control detected tetrachloroethene in the school, a chemical known to pose health risks for humans. During my observations, the county conducted an environmental study that determined that the tetrachloroethene present in the school was not strong enough to harm students, but could potentially pose a risk to teachers who had worked there for an extensive period of time.[8]

On my visit to Punta Vista School, I found the front door locked. I pushed a small black doorbell, and I was buzzed in a few seconds later. Cameras in the front lobby recorded my entry. The tall, husky, shaven-headed white security guard subtly lifted his head and wrinkled his face, as if to say, "What's up?" I returned his speechless gesture with a minimal response; tilting my head slightly to the side and lifting my chin, I said, "How's it going?"

As I arrived at the front office, the receptionist, a short, stocky middle-aged Latina with curly hair, was on the phone. She paused her conversation to ask, "How can I help you?" I explained I was there to see the principal, Ms. Mason, with whom I arranged my visit and classroom observations a few weeks prior.[9] Ms. Mason was a thin, dark-complexioned, middle-aged Latina who appeared to care for the students, but also demonstrated a "no nonsense" approach to dealing with discipline. During our first interaction in her office, she revealed, "Security. It's my favorite sport." Over time, I realized that her leadership approach was more concerned with preventing violence and crime at the school than educating students. The school structure and culture reflected this approach.

As I waited to see Ms. Mason, I observed the student check-in process. At the beginning of each school day, students lined up and presented all of their personal belongings to the front office staff: wallets, loose cash and change, cell phones, even their school supplies. Removing their shoes to ensure no weapons were hidden inside, the students were inspected with a handheld metal detector. The receptionist provided them a reference number—14, 15, 16, and so on—which they used after school to retrieve their belongings. Mark described his experience with the check-in process:

> This school's more controlled, we have no freedom. . . . It's like you come in and you checking in to prison but the teachers can't really control us. They just tell us what not to do. . . . They're so mad that they can't tell us what to do that they all they can do is tell us what not to do.

If a male student wore an extra-baggy shirt or a T-shirt with images considered inappropriate, security guards would give him a plain, bright-orange shirt to wear instead. One out of every five students ended up in this situation. I later learned that this bright-orange shirt also was used to punish students who defied school personnel, even if they were dressed appropriately. Clothing had become a contested symbol that authority figures used to control students' behavior and that students used to challenge the authoritarian order.

Mark saw the school's imposition of such strict control on students as a sort of unspoken compromise. Students would obey the disciplinary rules in exchange for lower academic expectations and requirements. This was a common theme in my observations of interactions between authority figures at Punta Vista. In its desperation to control unruly youths, the school exempted itself from serving its primary function—to educate—and instead defaulted to its secondary function—to keep these youngsters from breaking the law. In its practice and day-to-day interactions, the school operated as a quasi–criminal justice institution. Students understood this institution as a punitive one, and, as such, they informally agreed to follow its crime control rules and regulations, as long as they were not also required to fulfill its academic expectations. One might imagine the confusion and strain having to follow two sets of conflicting rules could have on young people—one from a criminal justice logic and one from an educational context. In the end, they negotiated with the institution to follow one set, while resisting the other. This might explain why so many of the students failed to return to the conventional high school or to make academic progress at the school. In our society, obsessed with a culture of control, obedience, law abidance, and regimentation become measures of success, good citizenship, and legality.

I waited nervously to meet the principal, swiftly shaking my leg as I felt chills tingle down my spine. Even for me, the overbearing presence of control imbued me with shame and foreboding. The feeling was eerily familiar, although the schools I attended never had this kind of intrusive check-in process. Later, reviewing my field notes for the day, I realized why I was so disturbed by the observation:

[handwritten margin note: conflicting rules – criminal justice logic / an education context –]

The staff at the school seems to look at the students with fear or disdain. The air feels thick with tension between staff and student. The staffs' eyes appear to dilate when they stare down the students, as if appearing to possess X-ray vision, giving the impression that they know every detail of a student's possessions and even knowing what a student is thinking. As one of the students, a short, chubby, square-headed, light-skinned boy by the name of Jaime walks in wearing a baggy black T-shirt, shaved head, and baggy dark-blue work jeans, and headphones, Mr. Juarez, a security guard, tells him, "I know you're in a bad mood today. Don't try to start anything or I will have to call your P.O. [probation officer]." Jaime has yet to mention a word. To me, he appears groggy from having just woken up. His eyes are droopy with a slight grin on his face as if saying, "I wish I was in bed right now" . . . he walks with a heavy slouch, hump on upper back showing, and a somber look. Watching students pass through this rigid, meat-packing-house-like, processing routine gives me the feeling of déjà vu—the school's check-in process is almost exactly the same as when I got booked into juvi.[10]

I was fifteen when I was incarcerated for the first time. Terrified, I experienced a check-in process much like the one at Punta Vista: My belongings were placed in a large plastic bag, and I was told to remove my clothes so my body could be inspected for illegal substances and contraband. I was then told to take a shower with a fluorescent-blue shampoo and body soap to "disinfect" myself and was given inmate garb to wear. The experience was humiliating, and I recognized that Punta Vista students went through a similar ritual—minus the shower—every time they walked through the door. Jorge found the process emasculating:

> I hate getting searched 'cause you have to get searched when you go inside . . . they tell you that you are their little bitch. They search you and I hate that. I don't like getting touched by another guy.[11]

≈ ≈ ≈ ≈

Eventually, Ms. Mason greeted me and escorted me to a classroom through hallways painted white with no decor, nothing at all to break up the stark institutional landscape. All classroom doors were closed, creating a claustrophobic feeling, as if the walls were caving in. Toward the very end of the hallway, a few wall posters advertised milk for healthy, lean, and muscular teenage bodies. On one of the posters, "model mom" Heidi Klum sat on a tall stool wearing a shiny evening dress that showed a large portion of her left leg. Her top lip was covered with a white "milk moustache."

[handwritten margin note: Contrast to FIHS]

I joined Mr. Jordan's class and found a seat in the back of the room. A video was playing, and students—sixteen Latino boys, five Latina girls, and one white girl—stared at the TV screen. Mr. Jordan, a stocky, middle-aged white teacher, was using the Olympics to illustrate his biology lesson. He had chosen the diving competition to explain concepts like rotation, revolution, and, in the case of two divers, the idea of synchronization. He also talked about how the Olympic judges scored the athletes. When the clip was over, Mr. Jordan turned off the television and asked what replication meant, specifically replication of DNA. A young man wearing an extra-baggy, blue-checkered dress shirt and sitting by himself in the very front responded, "It's like bootleg [pirated] videos." Mr. Jordan replied, "Yeah, but it doesn't have to be bad or illegal. Replication is a copy, a copy of anything."

In addition to the teacher, two security guards were in the room—Mr. Juarez and Mr. Thomas—one for every eleven students. They walked around the room to regulate behavior and ensure compliance. Mr. Juarez noticed two students resting their heads on their desks, so he walked up in front of them and tapped each on the shoulder—all while Mr. Jordan was trying to connect with the class about basic biological concepts. "Pay attention," the guard demanded in a stern, low, dragged-out voice with obvious frustration.

A video camera mounted high in a corner of the windowless room pointed toward the students, and below the camera a sign read, "Get glad, not mad." A blue Skechers shoebox had been converted into a "cuss box" and sat in front of the teacher's desk. "If you cuss, you pay ten cents, or stay in class ten minutes after school," Mr. Jordan whispered when he noticed me observing the box. This juxtaposition of creative attempts to socialize teenagers to behave themselves with that of rigid rules aimed at shutting down disruptive behavior and gang violence was a recurring theme at the school and in other settings in this study. Most authority figures attempted to create solutions for the issues that young people faced and the disreputable behavior they demonstrated. At the same time, when those attempts failed, they defaulted to a more punitive system of control that often directed the youths toward deeper, more formal sanctions. For example, Tito described a more antagonistic relationship with the teacher:

> Mr. Jordan tells you all right, if you don't want to learn that's fine with me, I don't give a fuck. I will still get paid the same. If you don't want to learn, that's your shit. You guys aren't going to amount to nothing. They [Mr. Jordan and other teachers] will tell you straight up: "If you guys don't want to do anything, just don't. . . . We don't care."

As Mr. Jordan lectured about DNA and how cells produced new copies of themselves, only three or four students were actively engaged. The others rested their heads on their desks—despite the constant policing against it—talked among themselves, or doodled on paper. Most students filled in the answers to their worksheets only after the teacher wrote them on the board, showing passive commitment to the classroom structures and an informal give-and-take in which they pretended to complete assignments as long as the teacher afforded them the answers.

Low morale abounded amid this vague semblance of teaching and learning. It was as if the youths were saying, "They pretend to teach me; I pretend to learn." This mutual affirmation of incompetence produced an environment in which students did the minimal amount of work to get by, and the adults focused on preventing violence and crime—nothing more. If the goal of schools like Punta Vista are to regulate behavior and reform students, they fail miserably because they have very little clue as to how cultural frames impact young people's actions and as to how punitive control often generates further resistance from young people, leading to unwanted, unruly behaviors.

Except for rare moments of frustration, Mr. Jordan appeared to want to help the students learn the rules that would help them get through school and, perhaps, survive in the real world that he defined according to the dictates of mainstream respectable behavior. His rules were flexible enough to accommodate those who did not know how to follow them, and he attempted to connect with his students at their level, although, ironically, some of these attempts simply served to shut down the students all the more.

Circulating around the classroom, Mr. Jordan stopped next to Matthew, a student sitting in front of me, and asked how his meeting with school district officials had gone. Matthew responded, "I am going back to the high school." Mr. Jordan replied, "So you earned the right to go back?" and then announced to the rest of the class,

> Matthew has earned his right to go back to the high school! That is what you all should be aiming for. You don't want to be stuck in this toxic pit for too long.

Many students were desperate to return to the conventional high school because they realized that being a student at Punta Vista degraded their image and cast them as social pariahs. Jorge described his attempts to return to the conventional school:

> Then I talked to the principal and she's like, "Well, yeah, you probably won't be able to go back. It's rare that a kid is able to go back after this and that . . . after being disrespectful to me and the teachers . . ." I remember one time I got suspended from this school, I don't remember why, but it was some *pendejada* [bullshit]. That stupid *pen-*

deja [idiot] told my dad, "I don't know why you bring your son; he should be in jail—life, for the rest of his life . . ." They never really teach: they always putting us down.

Continuing his stroll up and down the aisles, Mr. Jordan approached the back corner of the room where Mark was seated backward in his chair, punching the seat. Mr. Jordan asked,

What did the chair do to you? Did it pinch you in the keister? Please don't do that. Please turn back in your seat.

"Keister," meaning buttocks or "butt cheeks," had a double meaning, Mr. Jordan explained to me after class. According to Mr. Jordan, "keister" described the act of placing drugs or other contraband in one's anal cavity while in prison to hide them from authorities. Mr. Jordan had alluded to this process in class before, describing how some of his former students had ended up in prison and had to hide stuff in their "behinds." Mr. Jordan seemed to brag that he would know such things, as if being in the know might earn him street credibility with the students in class. In his attempts to connect with gang-associated boys at their level, Mr. Jordan used concepts he believed would be intimately familiar to them, such as keister. But Mark just looked perplexed. Later, when I asked Mark to explain the definition of keister, he said, "Butt? Shit, I don't know."

Authority figures commonly believed that they could gain an upper hand in regulating young people's behavior if they adopted a "play-it-cool" strategy to show they had some knowledge of street culture gained through contacts with older youths. "If I get to know who they are and how they talk," explained Mr. Jordan on one of my visits, "I find better ways at connecting with them." However, this perspective fails to consider the repercussions and ultimately misses the mark for establishing meaningful relationships with youths. I discovered that sometimes these well-intentioned teachers and police officers were actually teaching or affirming negative

[margin note: Repercussions for "play it cool" strategy]

frames and practices. At times, adults transmitted concepts that the boys were not yet familiar with, sparking their curiosity to explore things that they had no idea their older peers were engaged in. In this case, Mark was unfamiliar with "keister," the word or the act, but he developed a curiosity and a sense of embarrassment from not knowing an idea that was supposedly a part of street and prison culture.

In their attempts to reach young people, sometimes educators inadvertently socialize their students to accept the very disreputable behavior they seek to eradicate. This occurs because of the assumptions that educators make about these young people: that in order to reach them one has to approach them through street or criminal culture. The irony is that when young people respond with what is perceived to be street or criminal culture, authority figures react through stigma and harsh discipline.

As I observed at Punta Vista School, when authority figures dealt with disreputable youths, they applied the knowledge they learned from educational institutions and workplaces, social work, or criminal justice and began with positive interactions or attempts at positive interactions; yet, many times a punitive result ensued. Institutions produce interactions, policies, and programs aimed at connecting with youths to guide them, but ironically, these attempts to connect often result in processes that are not in the youths' best interests or well-being. As a result, these interactions represent negative institutional socialization, a process of inculcating counterproductive ideas, cultural practices, and behaviors that lead individuals to be rendered incompetent by institutions. Although with the positive intention of channeling normative behavior, and compliance, authority figures' language and actions end up causing students to disengage or misinterpret institutional expectations.

This incongruous outcome may have to do with the contradictory nature of formal and informal rules in schools. Formal rules maintain high expectations and rigid behavioral conduct, while informal rules allow for negotiation through which youths can act up as long as they don't trigger a sporadic, spontaneous negative reaction from a frustrated teacher, security guard, or administrator. I call this process as an *expectational contradiction* between adults and youths: The gang-associated youths are provided clear, rigid rules and expectations by teachers and administrators, and yet all parties engage in a more informal, flexible system of interaction, and adults and youth alike behave differently from how they may act outside of the confines of the institution. In this manner, both parties break the formal rules designed to educate or reform the youths and, thus, propagate the very behaviors and attitudes intended to be reformed. The culture of control seems to have as its main goal to regulate and control unruly behavior. The paradox here is that as control becomes a culture, it becomes inefficient at preventing or intervening in crime and instead produces resistance and magnifies transgressions, leading to a perceived sense of lawlessness.

At Punta Vista and across the landscape of similar institutional systems, expectational contradictions result in confusion, negative interactions, and high levels of uncertainty for marginalized young people. Youths at Punta Vista School did not know when they might be warmly welcomed, frigidly disrespected, or openly mocked for failing to navigate this ambiguous maze of rules and expectations. Therefore, when greeted in a positive manner, they responded with suspicion: "What are you trying to set me up to do now?" In this sense, the interactions between adults and youths fall flat. As authority figures default to negative interactions and punitive treatment to deal with youths' disrespectful behaviors, they reaffirm these young people's suspicions and mistrust of the institution and promote a self-fulfilling prophecy: Disreputable kids are defiant and need harsh punishment to learn their lesson. In turn, the school socializes young people through negative interaction that often results in additional negative repercussions in their future trajectories.

In his well-intentioned attempt to help students get by, Mr. Jordan, as an institutional representative, nudged young people like Mark to seek acceptance, dignity, and better interactions from another powerful institution, the gang. This negative institutional socialization encourages younger boys—the next generation—to seek out older boys on the street from whom they can learn about ideas and practices they first encounter through interactions with teachers and police officers. Harding (2010) called this phenomenon "cross-cohort socialization," younger boys in poor communities who seek older boys for teaching, guidance, and protection (see also Vigil 1988, 2002). Tito explained the role relationships with older boys had for him:

> I got into all this bullshit [getting in trouble with the law] 'cause I mean they [older boys] show love and shit . . . they showed me love. I seen them more like family you know? Like older brothers and shit.

These older boys are powerful in the lives of younger boys and socialize them in both positive and negative ways. Because the older boys are often involved in crime and unhealthy behavior, the younger boys can suffer negative consequences from these friendships, but, paradoxically, the older boys also can relay positive messages about life and education to their younger peers. For example, Justin explained his relationship with an older friend who was in jail but had been a strong role model:

> He's like twenty-three [years old]. He's looking at some crazy charges. He tells me to go to school and learn something. He tells me us Mexicans, like how we need more people educated and doing something and fighting for a cause that's right. Being oppressed and . . . people thinking we'll never amount to nothing. What he wanted to see was somebody to prove the system wrong . . . so in that sense he wanted me to go to school, if not for myself, then for that reason—to represent the hood in a positive way.

Mark also talked about learning to be an adult from older homies:

> I basically raised myself to be a man. And the way I could be a man, I learned from the homies and shit. Got to be down, got to be down for your shit, you know?

Although older boys could represent negative role models, I also found through several years of observation in Riverland that boys also encountered many opportunities for negative socialization in the institutions they navigated. As they developed from teenagers into adults, they absorbed countless messages from authority figures, messages that these young people interpreted as simply unpredictable and inconsistent. This confusing milieu led some to seek the stable predictability of a gang with its well-defined rules, structure, and functionality.

Although gang affiliation can bring negative social and health outcomes for young people, a gang as an institution sets clear formal and informal rules and predictable rules of engagement that require less emotional energy compared with socially sanctioned institutional structures. The gang also provides young people with their own brand of authority—senior gang members, sometimes only two to three years older—which resonates with their expectations for role modeling and counters their experiences of exclusion and stigmatization. Gang authority figures mean what they say in their interactions with the boys. In the gang, you either "put in work" or you don't; you snitch or you don't; you are loyal or you are not. Each of these binaries carries specific consequences: rewards for following the rules and punishments for not "being down." This transparency may be another central reason for the rock-solid social bonds among gang-associated boys.[12] Unlike the institution of the school, the institution of the gang accepts and embraces the multiple frames that young people embody. The gang, in many ways, has a more realistic, complex understanding of its members.

As the place that the community considered the "dumping ground" for "gang kids," Punta Vista was a laboratory in which to explore how the legal and education systems engaged, treated, socialized, and managed these youths. The case of Punta Vista is a prime example of how institutions charged with disseminating and monitoring a behavior of reform and compliance, ironically, can end up perpetuating criminality. Young people were inadvertently socialized to seek out or learn about street culture in two ways: In response to negative treatment from school authorities, youths were inclined to view street culture as a means of defiance or a way to reject the system, or youths interpreted adults' attempts to connect with them through a false sense of street cultural practices as disparaging them. In their attempt to comply, some students followed along, embracing these authority-imposed meanings and practices. This, in turn, affirmed their teachers' distorted understandings of them, constructing a reality dominated by institutional definitions of risk, reform, and control.

Some of the harshest punishments resulted from processes that appeared to be rooted in good intentions and creative, reform-based practices aimed at connecting with the boys. Adults would begin with a positive gesture with good intent, but as the interactions persisted, the continuum frequently would shift negative and both parties would end up attacking the other. For instance, during one of my observations, an English teacher initiated an interaction with a boy named Mike, asking simply, "How are you today?" Mike, a sixteen-year-old black and Latino youth with the build of a college football player, ignored her.

The teacher responded: "OK. You are choosing to ignore me. I hope you don't do the same with your in-class assignment." Annoyed, Mike replied, "I don't care about no assignment." The teacher retorted, "I will not take your attitude today." "Fuck, you are always lame. I didn't do shit," protested Mike.

At that point, the teacher crossed her arms, nodded her head toward the door, and without saying a word conveyed the message, "Leave my classroom." Mike stood up, grabbed his Texas Rangers baseball cap, and headed to the principal's office. How could such a seemingly innocuous and positive beginning deteriorate so quickly into a negative interaction? The teacher seemed to be making a positive attempt to reach out to Mike, and we could interpret this scenario as Mike's deliberate choice to ruin the moment and get into trouble.

However, on closer examination, the teacher's initial gesture—

"How are you today?"—set this positive-to-negative continuum in motion. The teacher mixed her greeting with body language that appeared cold. Her arms were crossed, and she looked at Mike with her mouth clenched and tension in her face that accentuated the crow's-feet above her cheekbones. Mike read the greeting as insincere, a mere formality in a process in which he was being set up to expel himself from the classroom. In a follow-up interview, he explained, "That white teacher is fucking scared of me. She always pretends to be cool, but her lame ass is setting me up."

Resistance to the culture of control had become part of Mike's cognitive process. He had developed a keen sense for reading physical and verbal cues exercised by authority figures and deciphering their intentions. As an observer, I could not know the teachers' intentions, but I did find a distinct difference between those teachers that Mike abhorred and those he liked. The teachers with whom Mike conflicted appeared diffident, tense, upset, or unsupportive in their body language or tone of voice when they attempted to reach out to him. In contrast, in classrooms where Mike presented himself as an attentive or compliant student, the teachers appeared relaxed, smiled often, and seemed happy to see their students, including Mike. Like many other youths I observed at Punta Vista and Riverland High School, Mike seemed to thrive with such adults. Positive verbal messaging alone is not enough. Students like Mike need authority figures to reflect on the informal messaging they engage in, including their body language.

From this English teacher's perspective, she was trying her best to connect with this young man, and she may have been unaware of the dissonant message her body language created. As far as she was concerned, she was trying to make Mike feel welcome in her class, despite their history of negative interactions. That was the best she could do. From Mike's perspective, he could read both words and body language, and he found a mismatch. Reading between the lines, Mike believed he could predict the teacher's next move: chastise him or send him out. In the end, even a positive gesture can conjure a cyclical set of actions and reactions: a negative response from youths, which produces justification for punitive treatment, followed by the stigma of criminality and gangs attached to youths. This process of rendering young people as human targets prevails in schools and among police, especially if they have been labeled as criminals and gang members.

Cultural Frames across Settings

Punta Vista was a space where young people with similar social and emotional needs were concentrated with little room for self-expression or positive development and where they were systematically stripped of their dignity on a daily basis. Besides not being conducive to learning, Punta Vista supported behaviors that compromised students' well-being and freedom through negative socialization, as youths based their respect for each other on their willingness to reject institutional practices.

With the best of intentions, Punta Vista School staff mimicked the students' cultural practices in an attempt to engage them. When this mimicking failed, authority figures defaulted to mocking youths' language and style—using slang words out of context, making fun of hairstyles and clothing, and pretending to act like students in order to exemplify how ridiculous their posturing looked to teachers. When cultural mimicking and mocking failed, school authorities relied on law-enforcement practices and resources to control the youths. But even the intervention of being removed from school could become a status symbol that demonstrated a youth's rejection of the institutional practices considered miserable, demeaning, and undignified.

An example of cultural mimicking was the practice of adults' appropriating the youths' vernacular when speaking to students, often with poor results. For instance, when adults used the word "lame," students often reacted with shrugged shoulders and dirty looks. Youths used the word "lame" to describe someone or something they didn't like or disapproved of: "That fool is a lame" or "This shit is lame." But in an encounter with some male students, Mr. Jordan used the word out of context and seemed to mock the boys when he said: "You are being lame—get back in the classroom."

Two boys looked at him and nodded, and one murmured under his breath, "*Ese pendejo* [that idiot] is the real lame."

Mr. Jordan's mistake was to neglect to add the article "a" before the word "lame," a distinction that indicated he did not really understand the students' world. In addition, he dragged out the pronunciation of lame, which seemed to mock some of the boys' speaking style; for instance, he interpreted traditional Southern California *cholo* (gangster) speak as "Hey homie, don't be a laaaame."

Interactions like these in which school authorities or police officers attempt to forge relationships, provide life lessons, or discipline youngsters are marred when adults' language and behaviors seem to reject, mock, mimic, replicate, or mirror youth culture. Indeed, these authority figures participate in the re/production of street culture and identity among disreputable young people, and worse, they seem to lack any self-awareness about the implications of their actions.

For example, Mr. Jordan would ask students, "What's going on out there? You got any new word to teach me?" On one level, he seemed to want to display genuine interest in the students' lives; however, once he interpreted and retransmitted words like "keister" or "lame," his interactions seemed at best awkward, irrelevant, or even offensive to students, and at worst sparked curiosity in the minds of younger students and normalized street behaviors. When I asked Mark about Mr. Jordan's use of slang, he said, "Mr. Jordan can say some nutty shit some times. But I sometimes think about, let me figure out, what he is saying just so I know."

On one of my observations at Punta Vista School, Mr. Jordan confronted Mark for ignoring him, and despite the teacher's attempt to act cool, Mark seemed unfazed by Mr. Jordan's request to turn around in his seat. At that point, Mr. Jordan pulled a candy from his pocket and handed it to Mark, who finally turned around and faced the front of the class for a few seconds. He then proceeded to scribble on his worksheet. A few minutes later, I glanced over to see what he drew: "thug life" in bubble letters with a shotgun hovering over it. Later that day, Mr. Jordan told me in passing, "If you want these kids to respect you, I recommend bringing some candy and giving them a piece when they start getting crazy."

As class came to an end, Juanita, a fifteen-year-old female student, excitedly slapped her palm on her desk as Mr. Jordan congratulated her for figuring out the answer to a question on the worksheet. She exclaimed, "I'm a star! I am going to college!"

Mr. Jordan's reply—"First, you need to go to 'normal' school," and "This is a school for backward individuals who have to earn back their rights"[13]—served to reinforce negative messaging and to drive students away from the very goals that school claimed to support.

The negativity and criminalization youth experienced from authority figures in one setting, such as school, translated to their being suspicious in other contexts. For instance, Jorge looked back in my direction and announced to another male student seated nearby, "Hey, they're watching you. They are taking notes on you dog." Another student said, "Really?" and turned to me, "Are you probation?" But my smile and the shake of my head did not belay his doubts: "You look straight up like probation, homie!"

As a bespectacled, early thirties college professor in loose (not baggy) jeans and polo shirts, I was consistently suspected of being a probation officer or an undercover police officer during my time in the field. But over six to nine months, these questions began to fade away. I doubt all of the boys ever trusted me completely, but at least they no longer questioned whether I was a law-enforcement officer or informant.

At the end of class, Mr. Jordan congratulated the group for participating, but focused his attention on the female students sitting at the front of the room. Mr. Juarez went around the room collecting pencils because students were not allowed to walk around school with them. The principal told me the reason for the rule was to avoid stabbings, "like in prison."

I asked, "How many times have students stabbed each other with pencils here?"

"None," she replied. "We're trying to keep it that way."

"How many times have students been stabbed with knives or other objects at the school?"

Again she said, "None, but we are trying to prevent it."

That exchange brought to mind the work of sociologist Robert Garot (2010), who argued that such preemptive harsh sanctions imposed by school officials on gang-associated students reinforce "tough identities." When schools center on managing and controlling students, the youth disengage from learning, which facilitates their adoption of a tough role, a process Garot labels the contradiction of control.

From Mr. Jordan's classroom, students transitioned to physical education, which consisted of walking around the school perimeter and the local neighborhood. When they returned to the school building, the students were subjected to another round of scrutiny and processing. Jorge was stopped by Mr. Juarez, who, referring to the loaner T-shirt meant to replace gang attire, told him, "Go grab a shirt." Jorge objected to wearing the shirt, and, after a three-minute debate, Ms. Mason, the principal, intervened, saying, "If you don't wear it, I will have to call your probation officer."

The principal regularly threatened students with calling their probation officers. For those not on probation, she threatened to call her brother, who was a sheriff's deputy in town. On two occasions, I witnessed police officers show up at the school after the principal called them regarding student misconduct. On any given day during the afternoon, for physical education hour, a group of about forty high school students could be seen walking around the neighborhood escorted by seven adults with radios, one holding a video camera. More than half of these students would be wearing baggy, bright-orange T-shirts, drawing perplexed stares from neighborhood residents, local business employees, and passersby. One day, I overheard a white woman sitting in a car remark, "Look at those poor kids in those god-awful prison outfits."

In his now classic work, sociologist Erving Goffman (1990) discussed different forms of stigma, some more visibly obvious than others. Those hapless enough to bear a stigma immediately apparent to others—what Goffman called a "stigma symbol"—garner troubling reactions from other members of society. Clearly, the bright-orange shirts were such a stigma symbol. Goffman noted that the public reacts with emotions ranging from terror to hatred to those who wear a stigma symbol. People may feel pity for the stigmatized, resort to abusive commentary, or organize to quarantine the stigmatized individuals away from society as if they festered with contagion.

At the end of each school day, Punta Vista students lined up to retrieve their personal belongings: cell phones, pencils, pens, folders, hats, cash, and keys. About five security guards were on duty in front of the school at dismissal—two at the right corner of the building, and three at the left. Mr. Juarez videotaped students as they left, "so that if they get into a fight, we catch it on tape," he explained.

Punta Vista School students and staff commonly referred to their environment as a jail or prison, and I discovered that this label was not simply a metaphor. The policies and restrictions of law enforcement and incarceration had penetrated this building very much like the tetrachloroethene found in the ground underneath the school.

≈ ≈ ≈ ≈

Two months after my first observation, Jorge was arrested at Punta Vista for threatening a teacher. He recounted what happened in a follow-up interview. I later confirmed his recollection with Mr. Juarez. One day, the teacher asked students to tell her their career choices. Jokingly, Jorge said, "I want to be a hit man when I grow up." Then he looked at her and said, ". . . and I want to start with you."

The teacher grabbed her cell phone, texted someone, and within twenty minutes, a police officer arrived to escort Jorge out of class for threatening the teacher and for violating probation. Jorge was released the following day, but was not allowed to return to school, nor was he given instructions as to where to report. With nowhere to go, for weeks he spent his entire day in front of one of his favorite hangouts, a neighborhood liquor store.

On the street, Jorge's day was now organized around avoiding arrest; police constantly impacted his daily routine in and out of school. In addition, he believed that he was targeted because of his race:

It could be a *guero* [white person] riding the bike on the sidewalk and I could be riding it as well, but they'll stop me and let that fool slide. They've done it in my face before. . . . It's like the *pinche* white kids get away with murder. They'll [the white kids] even admit it to you. *Te dicen que si ay racismo* [they tell you that there is racism]. They try to lock us up for anything.[14]

Criminologist Robert Durán (2013) argues that to understand the criminalization of Latino youths residing in the U.S. Southwest, we must understand the history of racialization and colonization. The boys in this study lived in a context in which their parents worked in precarious jobs tied to serving the elite class of Riverland. They labored in restaurants and in the construction industry, and as gardeners, babysitters, janitors, and housekeepers. The boys aspired to have jobs—even working-class positions—but were burdened with a criminal gangster stigma that diminished their ability to gain employment like their parents.[15] Within a generation, these Latinos had moved from being constructed as docile, cheap labor to a lazy criminal class needing punishment and confinement.

The youth I interviewed described the effects of this human targeting. When I asked Johny how he ended up at Punta Vista School, he told me,

I wasn't always bad. . . . When I got to junior high, there [was] honors and all this crap, and I was in those classes, too, and there were all these white kids and shit. I didn't really fit in, you know. It didn't really catch my attention as much, you know, like most classes and shit. So you know, I guess it was like just like, from right there, I was like, "fuck school."

I asked why he didn't fit in. "My teachers," he replied. "My teachers never gave a shit for me. They knew I didn't belong there 'cause of what I look like" (referring to his race and style).

Johny's aspirations were to join the military, but his dreams of joining the military were tainted by this experience: "Like I do want to go [to the Marines], but then I don't, because I'ma fight for a country that discriminates us and like thinks we are like shit."

Seventeen-year-old William had left school for similar reasons:

One time, I was in sixth grade, and I got in a fight with some white kid. I was the only one who got suspended, and that guy, they didn't even suspend him at all. I mean, he was right there fucking biting my leg and everything. Like seriously, that guy fucking dropped on the floor and started biting the shit out of my leg. I don't know what the hell, but that kid didn't get suspended at all, and I did. After that I said, "Fuck school."

Even as Punta Vista School staff members sought to change these gang-associated youths' behavior and set them on a more positive path, the youths could not escape being racialized human targets. Ironically, authority figures created the very conditions in which young people embraced negative frames, resisted control, and were emboldened to seek street life, by (mis)appropriation of their language or style, mocking the youths and their culture, and resorting to a system of confusing informal rules and punitive responses. Instead of promoting positive cultural frames—going to college, staying legit, forming healthy relationships—the informal inter-actions at the school all too often reinforced street-life frames that led youngsters deeper into trouble. Surprisingly, authority figures seemed to lack any self-awareness about how their actions, behav-

iors, and language contributed to a system of expectational contradictions and student failure. To escape being human targets, young
people sought refuge from stigmatization in subcultures where they,
not only could resist marginalization, but also created alternative
spaces in which to express and practice the full complexity of their
identities. One of these places of belonging was on the streets, in
front of the local liquor store. Here, gang-associated youths enjoyed
a command and communication center, a respite, and a perceived
protective factor. But they also drew the watchful attention of the
Riverland police. *creation of a alternative spaces for students to resist strongly embedded culture of control over them*

CHAPTER TWO

The Liquor Store and the Police

The pavement outside of Golden State Liquors, in the heart of the south side, served as a main hangout for some of Riverland's gang-associated boys. The small, shack-like building was the size of a shipping container, with one two-by-four-foot window covered by metal bars. A mismatched khaki-colored paint job was chipping off the building's facade. Graffiti bled through rectangles of darker shades of paint slapped on to cover the letters "SSL," for South Side *Locos*, and monikers like "Joker" and "Tweeker." Above the store entrance, a small sign painted in faded green letters read, "Golden State Liquors. We Carry Indian Groceries," although I never once located ethnic Indian food items on any of the several occasions I browsed the store.

Golden State Liquors was a perfect archetype of the poor, urban neighborhood market. Conveniently located on the corner of a central street, the store offered a variety of junk foods; a handful of old, bruised tomatoes, bananas, and lemons; and one refrigerator full of sodas and other sugary drinks. About a fourth of the store was dedicated to alcohol products: Four old, noisy, aluminum and glass refrigerators were stocked with tall cans and forty-ounce bottles of malt liquor and American beer. One shelf boasted an array of two-dollar bottles of California wine.

Outside, broken Christmas lights dangled over a quarter of the building, and two skeletal pay phones sat useless, their receivers missing. A Glacier water vending machine was situated at the outside corner of the building. Despite the trash, gum, and stains from beverages and urine that covered the store sidewalks, the water vending machine was clean and intact, and neighborhood mothers and grandmothers regularly frequented it to fill water jugs. In sixty-five observations here, I witnessed vandalism and loitering everywhere on the property, except the water dispenser. One of the boys explained that the water dispenser was for *jefitas*—benevolent, revered mothers—to use to nurture their families. The water dispenser was off limits; no one was to vandalize it.

Golden State was a principal gathering point for the boys I followed, an important site where many spent the majority of their leisure time. There, they convened, caught up with each other, and talked about life, probation, girls, kids, school, and work. Golden State served as a communication hub where they planned group activities together, with one wall of the building serving as a message platform. Whenever a friend died, the boys spray-painted "RIP" on the wall to honor him, and the storeowner respectfully waited several days before painting it over in another shade of khaki.

While the liquor store could serve as a cauldron for risky, health-compromising behaviors, it also was one of the only spaces in South Riverland where the boys said they were respected and treated fairly by an adult, the storeowner.

The owner, Abjit, a South Asian American man in his fifties, greeted the boys politely by name, occasionally sparking long conversations with each of them. He asked them about their families and whether they planned to go back to school. Abjit ended most conversations with "OK, man, please try not to make too much of a mess out here."

He willingly ignored the boys' trash and minor vandalism because, he told me,

> They're children. I don't blame them. This is their community. I am a visitor. If my home [store] can make them feel comfortable, then I have an obligation to help them. I get tired of painting the wall and cleaning up after them, but they protect my store. They don't steal from me, and they keep the corner safe.

In an unspoken give-and-take, Abjit put up with loitering and lit-
tering and provided a space for the boys to call their own in exchange
for their keeping more harmful transgressions like theft, drug dealing, and violence at bay. Abjit viewed these young men as "children"
who needed his intense guidance and emotional support. This perspective was quite different from that of the majority of teachers
and police officers I had encountered, who assigned these youth the
capability of reasoning and acting as adults and held them accountable for their behaviors as they would adults. This process of "adulti-
fication" occurs differently for children from low-income families
than for those from higher-income homes. For the children of the
poor, acts that may be treated as childish and minor for wealthier
children are considered—and prosecuted—as criminal.[1] One dominant strategy for attempting to regulate negative Latino youth behavior in Riverland was to create a rigid system of unrealistic expectations. Adolescents had to behave and be held accountable as
rational, responsible adults. If they broke any rules, their deviance
was immediately targeted by authority figures. This created a racialized deviance amplification process in which skin color determined
the ways in which adolescent behavior was policed. If you are young
and brown, your actions, style, and transgressions are placed under
deep scrutiny.

In contrast to the targeting and distancing attitudes of schools
and police, Abjit understood the social order of the neighborhood,
and he participated in the cultural milieu that young people brought
to his store. This provided him the opportunity to maintain order
in and around his store. For the most part, the boys kept their end
of the bargain with Abjit. Fights and drug deals occurred in other
spaces, the creek, the park, and other street corners, and beer runs—
grabbing a case of beer and running out without paying, a regular
practice among the boys—were committed elsewhere. The boys and
Abjit had forged a connection, and a reciprocity developed from Abjit's desire to support them.

"I know that if I call the police they will just lock them up and
when they come out I will have to deal with them again and again—

they just need a place to talk," Abjit explained. Self-interest surely provided an incentive for Abjit's tolerance, I thought. After all, the boys' families were loyal customers of his store and allowed his business to thrive. But Abjit rejected any suggestion of ulterior motives and insisted his attitude was not about the money, but about being "humane." Unlike many other adults and authority figures, Abjit refused to target the boys as gangsters and criminals. He saw them for what they were—multidimensional human beings. As a result, the boys considered Abjit a supporter, someone who understood them in their full complexity, and in return they showed care and empathy for his property and his customers. There was a deep irony in the fact that a liquor store owner appeared more literate in understanding young people's multiple frames than most authorities at Punta Vista School or police officers. This immigrant liquor store owner saw the potential that these young people had to offer. He was one of the few people in the community that changed his understanding of these young people from seeing their presence as a threat to seeing their presence as an asset: they helped to maintain the local order, even if at a microscale.[2]

Outside of the school, Golden State Liquors was where I met most of the other boys in this study. I gained introductions to them through Jorge and Mark. "This is the guy writing about us," Jorge told them, vouching for me as a college teacher unaffiliated with law enforcement. Still, many of the young men questioned my presence, suspecting me as a probation officer or a police informant. Sometimes, they walked away from me murmuring curse words, calling me a "lame." Other times, they directly confronted me, asking again and again if I was a police or probation officer. Initially, on four occasions, I was pushed, threatened, and told that if I were lying, I would "get fucked up." Each time, I responded that I was not police or probation, but a college professor studying the experiences of young people growing up in that neighborhood who wanted to learn about their experiences with schools, the streets, and police.

On one of the initial days that I visited Golden State Liquors, I found twelve young men, five of whom I already knew. One of the new ones—a chubby, bald man of perhaps twenty—drove up on a shiny, stainless-steel beach cruiser with extra-long handlebars. Perched next to me, he said nothing, so I introduced myself and asked him his name. I had committed my first mistake: asking him his name before he knew if I was trustworthy. He replied, "Wilson. My name is Wilson." That was not his name, but one he made up because he didn't trust me. Later, he revealed his true name, but I have kept the pseudonym he created for this naive researcher.

As I talked to Wilson, a group of about six boys gathered around us. I told them about my previous research project in Northern California; they seemed intrigued. Without revealing too much information that might influence their answers later on, I told them some of my findings:

> You know, I have found that young people try really hard and that sometimes it takes some help to get places. . . . How about police? How do the police treat you here?

They all lit up, and Wilson replied, "They're fucked up out here, ay. They search us, grab on us all nutty, take us to jail for nothing, handcuff us, and sit us on the ground for days." That is exactly what I wanted to know: their firsthand, unfiltered accounts of experiences with institutions and authority figures. The boys agreed that I could keep talking to them, and from that point forward and over the next five years, I showed up at least twice a week to observe and interview them.

Later, my students and I started a weekly workshop at a local community center, El Centro, and invited these boys to participate in focus groups about the issues they faced. I figured that the best way to keep tabs on such an evasive population—constantly shifting between places of residence and in and out of juvenile hall, jail, or prison—was to provide a space with a specific day and time for them to check in, partake in focus groups, and have a meal. While we conducted the research component, the community center staff coordinated services that might benefit the youths. In collaboration with the community center, I invited different community workers and community members to discuss culture, politics, employment, and higher education—all of the issues that truly mattered to youths marginalized by the very institutions that were supposed to serve them.

There, I walked a fine line between systematically and transparently studying these young men's lives and subjectively providing support, which could, in turn, change their trajectories and perspectives. To deal with this dilemma, I distanced myself from the community center's interventions with the youths and, instead, selected a control group of six boys whom I would purposely and directly attempt to help. Thus, I could test how my own participation and that of my students as additional authority figures might influence these boys' perspectives and trajectories. Instead of covering my eyes and pretending there was no elephant in the room, I acknowledged the bias and subjectivity of my hankering to help these boys as I observed the mistakes they made and the stigmatization and criminalization they encountered. At the same time, there were many young people that I wished I could help, but, in my limited capacity, I simply shadowed them to observe their trajectories.

Establishing trusting relationships with these young people presented many challenges. Because they lived in constant fear of arrest, I had to prove to these young men that I would not "rat them out" with the police. Later, I observed firsthand the police harassment, brutality, and entrapment that spawned this. I had to reassure the youths that our conversations were confidential; they were not even required to reveal their identities, and if the police somehow acquired the data, they would not be able to connect names to transcriptions. In addition, my research group and I initially avoided conversations or relationships with the police, except for the police chief, whom I later interviewed in an effort to understand the rampant police misconduct that the youths reported and I eventually observed. On the advice of the youths in the study, I delayed riding along with the police Gang Suppression Team because they thought it would look suspicious. Once I had ended my formal observations with the youths at the end of the study's fourth year, a graduate student colleague of mine, Samuel Gregory Prieto, and I conducted ride-alongs to observe Riverland youths from the police officers' perspective (see chapter 5).

My interactions with the boys were awkward during those early encounters. When I showed up on the street corner and approached them, they walked away and maintained a distance; some left the corner altogether. As I persisted, they became used to me, and although they continued to be cautious about what they talked about around me, they began to accept my presence.

Another challenge to establishing genuine relationships with these young people was the myriad of behavioral and circumstantial issues they faced, which surfaced during our meetings. Some arrived to interviews or focus groups high on drugs or alcohol or angry about something that had happened on the street or in the classroom. In the beginning, on many occasions, they made disrespectful remarks. For example, during a focus group session at the local community center, Pedro, a twenty-one-year-old recently released from a thirty-two-month prison term for assault with a deadly weapon, showed up drunk and raring to pick a fight. Discussing masculinity with the boys, I asked, "What makes a man, a man?" Pedro jumped at the chance to tell his story and spread some advice. For five minutes he spoke passionately, yielding to no one:

> Just be down, just hold your ground, don't do bitch shit like what we talked about; don't be fake, don't talk about it, be about it. If you want something, go get it. Don't just be yipping and yapping, 'cause then that's all you are—talk . . .

After he repeated the same remark for the third time, I interrupted and reminded the group about taking turns speaking.

"Man, I am not done talking, fool!" Pedro exclaimed.

Another guy, Roger, countered, "He's a doctor, fool!"

"And I'm a convicted felon. I don't give a fuck! You know my respect comes from where his respect came from?"

"Yeah, but he's smart though, fool," Roger replied.

"Let that fool get ten years to twenty-five years to life. Who's smart then? . . . Yeah, I started talking first! And he's just like, oh, let's go to the next guy. . . . Let's not listen to the bald guy [referring to his shaved head]; let's listen to the guy with hair!"

At that point, Pedro stood up, looked me in the eyes and admitted, "I'm a pretty short-tempered guy."

I calmly remained in my place, placing my open hands together about six inches from my face, and asked. "'*Spensa* [short for *dispensa*, "sorry" in Spanish], man, what can I do to make things better?" Pedro pointed to Ismael, a friend of mine and gang prevention worker that was visiting the focus group sessions, and said, "I want the guy with the braids [referring to Ismael's braided long hair]; he will be easier on me . . . that fool's like chill." Ismael, who had established a relationship with Pedro, took him to another room to talk. An hour later when I checked on them, they were telling jokes and talking about a birthday party Pedro was planning to attend that evening. Pedro had come to understand me as yet another authority figure, shutting down his voice, demanding that he follow the rules. I had personified the very targeting authority that I had come to study. And in this moment, I empathized with teachers and police officers who in simply trying to ask a question had come to be seen as punitive, disrespectful villains robbing young people of their dignity. I realized how easy it could be to generate negative interactions with marginalized young people when seen as an authority figure. This occurred because the conventional understanding of authority figures is that they are there to overpolice the compliance to follow norms and rules. Disreputable young people develop a resistance to this interactional overpolicing, while authority figures develop a counterresistance that further diminishes the social fabric of interactions and relationships. In attempting to maintain order, authority figures often forget about the most basic factors that dictate young peoples' circumstances, attitudes, and behaviors.

≈ ≈ ≈ ≈

As I continued my observations on the street corner, I discovered that the boys regularly talked about being hungry, searching for some cash to buy snacks like potato chips or a donut. Oftentimes, I showed up after five o'clock at the liquor store, and one would tell another, "Man, I haven't eaten all day." I wondered if talking about hunger was a ploy to gain my sympathy so I would hand over some money; but none of the boys ever asked me for money. Contrary to popular belief that "gangster boys" are money-hungry, I found that many were simply hungry. I came to find that even small meals and small financial resources could meet the basic needs of these marginalized young people and might shape their interactions and behaviors and even prevent them from getting into trouble.

One day, I decided to bring food—a bucket of Kentucky Fried Chicken—as a way to offer a little sustenance to youngsters who were physically hungry, but also to forge a connection with them and gain their trust. When I walked up and offered some chicken to three boys on the corner, they looked at me with a suspicious, puzzled gaze. I walked the bucket over to a set of steps adjacent to the liquor store, announced that the food was there if they wanted some, and returned to the corner.

Jorge looked around to see if anyone was watching, pulled up the legs of his baggy pants, and walked cautiously toward the bucket of chicken. He looked to his left, straight ahead, and behind him, before swiftly grabbing a chicken leg and taking a massive bite. By the time he had returned to the corner, he was holding a greasy bare bone. He tossed it onto the curb. It bounced a few times and landed in the middle of the street. Following Jorge's lead, the other two boys walked over and grabbed a piece. Jorge wiped his hands on his pants and pulled out his cell phone to text someone, murmuring, "I gotta tell the homies we got some chicken here, dog."

Ten minutes later, a group of four approached. They shook my hand, enacting a uniquely Southern California four-step handshake that begins with a conventional grip, moves to an upward rotation allowing one to grasp the top of the other's hand, then a pulling gesture on each other's clenched fingers, and finally punching fists together. While this shake is now common in Southern Californian youth culture, it has been historically practiced by Chicano youth in working-class neighborhoods. The boys walked over to the chicken, proceeding to "tear it up." Twice I heard the familiar phrase: "I haven't eaten all day."

≈ ≈ ≈ ≈

In the shadow of Golden State Liquors, the boys caught up on neighborhood news, relaxed, and found refuge in this supportive space co-created with Abjit. There, they could buy snack foods and beverages, often their only meal, purchased with whatever money trickled in throughout the day, from those who might appear with fifty cents or a couple of dollars. All under twenty-one, the boys could not legally purchase alcohol, but occasionally they would pay a transient to buy it for them—but not from Golden State. Abjit usually refused to sell alcohol to transients, knowing that the boys would end up drinking it. His policy indicated that while he was lenient and supportive with the boys, he was also willing to take a stand when it came to compromising activities. But the boys found alternatives. They traveled to other neighborhood liquor stores to buy booze or set up a beer run. For a majority of boys in the study—thirty-one out of fifty-six—their first arrest was the result of a beer run.

Golden State Liquors served as an alternative site for the boys to collectively develop, deploy, and reinforce particular cultural practices. On that corner, older boys served as authority figures for younger boys and taught them how to carry themselves on the street. They provided a sense of security, even as, in some instances, they guided them in the wrong direction. Mark explained his perspective on the liquor store and the relationships the boys built and affirmed there:

> The way like cops and society see it, they see it [gangs] as like a group whose number one objective is like commit crimes and like cause chaos like that's their thing. But I don't see it like that. Like all the

homies, as they call them, they're my friends, they're who I grew up with, so it's like we all grew up into the gang, like that's what was around. So I don't see it as a gang, I see it as a friendship . . . the liquor store guy, he knows what we are about. He has seen us since we were kids. That fool's a homie too! He sees us as the friends we are—like that's how everybody should see us.

Law enforcement did not share the boys' view of the street corner at Golden State Liquors as a space of affirmation, recreation, and support; to them, the corner was a criminogenic location in need of intense policing. Why such a differential understanding? For one thing, police officers and youths viewed each other through very different lens: Police acted toward youngsters based on a potential threat perspective and their desire to prevent crime, while gang-associated youths' perspectives on the police obfuscated any gestures of support or positive interactions. As a result, interactions between police and youths often turned negative.

Similar to the adults at Punta Vista School, police officers drew upon their training and good intentions to approach gang-associated youths, but as their interactions increased, their positive gestures faded away and negative comments and treatment emerged. In part, the youths acted in ways that drew the officers' more negative treatment because they believed the initial positive gestures were disingenuous and artificial. Their attitude seemed to be reflected by Mark's assertion during an interview, "No need to fake it officer. You don't like me, I don't like you. . . . Just search me and get it over with. Save the hellos for the *gueros* [white people]." Officers responded to this demeanor with terse, often undignified treatment, which, in turn, extracted blatant and extreme reactions from the youths.

This same miscommunication generated conflicting perspectives on the liquor store. For the boys, the location was a sanctum and a place to show decency and respect for the sake of security, familiarity, and friendship. In this safe zone, they could congregate under an unwritten rule that acts of criminality were off-limits. But for police—and some neighborhood residents—that very space was where gang crime was conspired, and the mere presence of gang-associated youths provoked anxiety and heavy policing. Officers typically failed to see the social control that the store maintained for the boys. Once scattered, the boys were more likely to engage in crime and to be victimized. In this sense, the liquor store did serve as a protective factor: it created a pocket of viable, sustainable order that young people could genuinely agree to while fulfilling their adolescent desires—to hang with the homies.

Cultural Misrecognition and Strategies of Drift

Tonyo, who was sixteen when Jorge introduced him to me in front of Golden State Liquors, was adept at shifting his demeanor, attitude, and language based on the setting. Around his friends he was low-key, minimally engaging in conversation. Typically, he was the first to go home after sunset because, he said, "I know when stuff gets nutty. I know when people get stabbed, when fools start to tweek [use methamphetamine], and when people get arrested. It all happens after dark." Tonyo's strategy was to show face with his friends so they knew he was still "down" with being part of the gang, but to get out of the way when negative encounters with police and rival gangs were more likely.

At least twenty of the boys I studied reported a desire to leave crime and gang life behind, but needed to prove they were still "down" for fear of peer rejection and retaliation. Like Tonyo, most young men who wanted to leave gang life embraced resources and positive interactions with adults at school and at the community center. Tonyo's goal was to leave the gang eventually and reconnect with his one-year-old daughter: "I want to change, be somebody positive, move to Arizona, be a family man with my girl." He sought work to save enough money to make the move, and in the meantime, he remained in school in hopes of receiving a GED, high school–equivalency diploma.

Two different times I observed police questioning Tonyo at the park, asking him what he was doing there and if he had drugs on him. Both times Tonyo did not respond, and both times the officers became aggravated and proceeded to handcuff him and place him in the patrol car. Still, Tonyo would not speak a word to police officers. On one of these occasions, the officers arrested him for vandalism, claiming he "tagged" a building down the street a few hours earlier.

When I asked Tonyo why he would not speak to the police in his own defense, he said, "I'm just trying to show that I got nothing to hide. If I talk, they might think I am telling them a lie and then they'll try to set me up." Tonyo reported feeling "fucked up" and "like shit" when officers did not understand his silence as his attempt to avoid getting in trouble. In Tonyo's worldview, the police officers believed everything he said was a lie. To remain silent might upset the officers—certainly a palpable risk—but from Tonyo's perspective, silence also minimized the officers' abilities to find contradictions in his statements. Unfortunately, this tactic drastically escalated the already adversarial relationship between Tonyo and the police as both parties viewed the other with indifference and disrespect.

Two months after I began to follow Tonyo, the FBI and local law enforcement kicked in his family's apartment door and pulled handguns and assault rifles on him and his mother, fifteen-year-old sister, cousin, older brother, and sister-in-law. Everyone was taken outside, put in patrol cars, and interrogated about Tonyo's alleged drug sales and gang conspiracy. Tonyo and his brother were arrested. His family later showed me photos of the aftermath: overturned beds, pillaged closets, and dresser drawers scattered throughout the apartment.

At the same time, more than four hundred FBI and local law-enforcement officers had raided many other homes in this and one other local working-class Latino community in a crackdown on an alleged organized crime enterprise in the region. Along with Tonyo and his brother, over fifty other alleged gang members were arrested with charges ranging from drug sales to racketeering. Many individuals were indicted by a federal grand jury under the Racketeer

Influenced and Corrupt Organizations Act (RICO), originally developed to target mafia organizations.

Tonyo's fifteen-year-old cousin, a boy nicknamed Silent, was staying at Tonyo's house when the raid occurred and described the experience:

> It was like five, six in the morning, and they like, I don't know, I just remember like all kinds of bangs and like screams and like I couldn't understand what they were saying so I just remember jumping out of my bed and I went. . . . I thought it was somebody like, like from the rival gang you know and they got everybody on the ground and even like my aunt. It was the feds like. I was tripping out they were like in ski masks and like, like suited and hooded and like all . . . after, they pointed a gun over my aunt's head who got on the ground. . . . Like right after [the raid], I would have like, like nightmares, like I had to see a counselor at my school, 'cause like they noticed that I slept not enough, like you're too jumpy and act weird after. Even now [one year later], I wake up and like, like jump up and thinking that the cops are right there. I have like visions in my head, and like, last time they come to my house . . . the cops are following me.

Tonyo was compelled to sign a plea deal, based on a video recording showing him standing beside his friend as the friend sold an undercover police officer an eighth of an ounce of methamphetamine, worth about $200. The police maintained that Tonyo was a lookout for the gang and the transaction was conducted to benefit the gang. Under threat of serving up to ten years in federal prison if he did not take the deal, Tonyo signed the plea and served nearly two years. While serving his sentence, he wrote about his experience with authority figures in a letter from prison:

> If I could go back in time to when I was fourteen, fifteen, I had been all confused. I needed someone, a role model, a father figure, someone to guide me the right way. But the teachers and police that I talked to, they all gave me shit. So I just hated them.

Indeed, based on the interactions I observed between Tonyo and police, these adults clearly misrecognized Tonyo's attempts at "staying out of trouble." They seemed to believe he was being defiant when he was trying to avoid being incarcerated, or as he understood it, being "set up."

After being released from prison, Tonyo regularly attended meetings, focus groups, and programs at El Centro. He took advantage of job and counseling opportunities and was one of the first young men to complete applications and make appointments with social workers to discuss his problems and the resources he could tap. Over a six-month period, I observed him working hard at his goal: obtain employment and save enough money to move to Arizona to be with his daughter. A few weeks later, he was hired to prepare bouquets at a florist. He worked there for seven months, and hung out with his friends very minimally, two to three hours on weekends.

Tonyo's behavior at the community center was cordial and respectful. His interactions with the staff were substantive, meaningful, and respectful, very different from his terse interactions with police officers. What was it about the quality of the interactions between Tonyo and the community center staff that enabled him to open up and engage positively with them? I believe the answer lies in the combination of Tonyo's desire to access resources to help him accomplish his goal and the community center staff members' ability to view him with genuine respect. At the community center, Tonyo felt safe, and he acted accordingly, speaking openly and respectfully about his aspirations.

Eventually, Tonyo saved enough to move to Arizona. But when he sought permission from his parole officer to move out of state, the officer denied his request, claiming that Tonyo wanted to move only to expand the gang's enterprise. Soon after the denial, Tonyo told me he felt "messed up," and I noticed him drinking with his friends twice that week following the denial.

Two weeks later, as Tonyo was again drinking with three of his friends, a man who had clashed with his friends walked by the park where they were hanging out. Two of the guys began to attack the man; Tonyo stood there, watching the brutal beating. The man later died at the hospital.

Despite Tonyo's "snitching" on his friends, the friends' confession to the crime, and their attesting to Tonyo's innocence, Tonyo is serving sixteen years in prison, six years for voluntary manslaughter and ten years for an added gang enhancement—an extra sentence typically granted to crimes committed "for the benefit of the gang."

Although Tonyo played a major role in carving out his own destiny, his attempts to improve his outcomes and seek a productive life were consistently shut down through authority figures' cultural misrecognition. His probation officer failed to understand Tonyo's genuine attempts to improve his life; police claimed his refusal to answer their questions was proof that Tonyo was conspiring with the gang, and they placed his name in a gang database that eventually would saddle him with an additional ten years of imprisonment for a "gang enhancement"; and his school considered him a serious threat, expelling him at a young age for a "gang fight." Piled one on the other over a number of years, these deleterious interactions set Tonyo on a life course toward hard time in prison.

Sociologist David Matza (1964) argues that juvenile delinquents navigate between two extremes, constantly drifting from conventional to criminal behavior. He finds that the guilt young people feel after committing a crime compels them to seek balance and to return to law-abiding behavior. Then, after desperation and preparation, they reoffend. Initially, the will to commit a crime is activated from the desperation that arises out of some extraordinary occasion or fatalism, the feeling of having no control over one's surroundings. Injustice is a central activator for this drift between conventional and criminal behavior. When youngsters feel they are treated unjustly, their connection to law-abiding behavior is eroded.

Glen Elder's (1985) concepts of transitions and trajectories enhance this idea of drift. Elder compares young people's transitions (a specific sequence of events based on age) with their trajectories (pathways in life, such as high school graduation), and finds that certain juvenile subcultures include transitional cultural experiences that, in turn, affect long-term life trajectories for drifting juveniles. One example is Tonyo's transitional experience of showing his peers that he could live a street-life cultural frame as part of being a man on the street. Despite wanting to flee the scene of a drug sale or the scene of a brutal beating, he believed he had to prove to his peers that he was very much a man by not taking off. This transitional experience impacted his trajectorial experience because the criminal justice system and the law intervened in his ability to repair these mistakes.[3]

Contexts—specifically, the quality of interactions within institutional settings—impact this drift and transitional and trajectorial experiences. In my observations of Tonyo and other youths in various settings, I could see how each setting elicited a different kind of persona in the youths. The prominent urban ethnographer Ulf Hanners (2004), who studied working-class African Americans in Washington, DC, argued that the lifestyles of marginalized populations (like all demographic groups) are differentiated and diverse, and roles and types are fluid. He defined lifestyle as "the involvement of an individual with a particular set of modes of actions, social relationships, and contexts." In this way, we can think of a lifestyle not as a fixed type, but rather a temporary engagement, as a person hooks into a certain set of cognitive processes and actions within certain social interactions.

Negative interactions with authority figures can spur gang-associated youths to temporarily adopt defiant and criminal "lifestyles" (Hagedorn 1988; Vigil 1988), and, likewise, understanding these processes can help identify interactions and contexts that can influence delinquent youths to desist from gang and/or criminal activity.

Tonyo and many of the other boys in South Riverland experienced a misrecognition of interactions and interpretations across various community settings. Cultural misrecognition occurred when authority figures failed to understand or acknowledge a young person's genuine attempts to abandon crime and engage in school or the labor market. When the boys displayed a genuine interest in "going legit," authority figures sometimes interpreted their statements and efforts as rude or malicious acts. The young men attempted to adopt the cultural frames of respectability and morality they learned in their homes and neighborhood, and in certain contexts, like their families and peer groups, these frames were understood as positive and appropriate. But in other settings, like school and the labor market, these same cultural frames were considered deviant or malicious. This important distinction underscores that cultural framing and heterogeneity cannot be understood without also understanding institutional context and power. Individual action, or agency, is heavily impacted by how institutions read, react to, and interact with specific cultural frames. When institutions criminalize or neglect specific frames and promote other frames, they inadvertently set an agenda for inclusion of specific individuals and exclusion of others. In the case of the south side boys, multiple institutions had neglected, rejected, or penalized specific cultural practices.

≈ ≈ ≈ ≈

I witnessed police harass another seventeen-year-old male, Mono, three times over the course of a year and a half. In one incident, my graduate students and I were hanging out on the street in front of El Centro community center with Mono, who wore a thick moustache and had a shaved head, when he pulled out a cigarette from his pocket. A police officer drove up and addressed Mono, "You got ID?"

As Mono nodded yes, the officer demanded, "Pull it out then!"

The officer handcuffed Mono and sat him on the ground for over forty minutes while he checked his record and waited for other officers to arrive. When I asked the officer why he stopped Mono, he replied, "He just looked suspicious." During the five years of fieldwork, I counted seventy-four similar negative interactions.

Negative interactions with police were not limited to young males. Eight out of the eighteen young women whom we interviewed also reported such experiences. Though less common than for boys, those girls caught up in the street life also faced ubiquitous punitive treatment by schools and police. Shorty, a seventeen-year-old Mexican American girl, told us why her arm was in a cast: "The cops tackled me down because they thought I was going to run after a fight that I had with some girl. . . . I messed up my arm and had to go to the hospital because of the tackle." Other young women reported incidents when police searched and groped them and said police had called them "bitches" and "gang whores."

Police also sometimes played a role in street politics and, like the Punta Vista teachers, crossed the line into negative institutional socialization. Miguel explains his experience with police attempts to incite gang fights:

> Cops also try to provoke us sometimes . . . like if someone from the [north] side did something to our people. . . . They will say something like, "Aren't you going to go do something about it?"

In the shadow of Golden State Liquors, the gang-associated boys found a safe zone that allowed them to find affirmation and refuge and to communicate with each other and network. Moreover, the street left them exposed to criminalization, police harassment, and incarceration, bearing labels that targeted them as dangerous, potential criminals.

CHAPTER THREE

Cultural Misframing

(with Patrick Lopez-Aguado)

For gang-associated Latino youths in Riverland and at Punta Vista School, *cholo* style—a shaved head, baggy clothes, and visible tattoos—portrayed one dominant identity. *Cholo* can be translated as "gangster," but that is imprecise, as the meaning is more nuanced than that. *Cholo* also refers to a larger subculture that dresses and acts in ways that some may perceive as thuggish or gangster-like; however, certain Latino communities embrace the idea of *cholo* precisely because it is not associated with crime and violence, but rather with a youthful, temporary, caricaturized identity.[1] Family and community members may mock or ridicule youths for their style, but condone it because, often and for the most part, it isn't a threat to anyone—it's just that, a style. Some community members have a complex and fairly accurate understanding of youths who gravitate toward *cholo* culture. They believe that this is a temporary and fluid identity. Youngsters will adopt *cholo* culture to get away, for leisure, to feel empowered. However, schools and law enforcement don't understand this complex identity and instead label *cholo* style as criminal style. After police and schools convince parents about their children's criminality, many youth also experience shame from their parents, which can turn the family into another institution of criminalization (see Rios 2011).

Previous to police or school labels, *cholo*, like "punk" subculture, is not necessarily associated with crime among parents and relatives of youths. Young people who dress in a punk style and listen to punk music might garner derision from older community members, but they are not necessarily considered criminal conspirators. In this sense, community members understand *cholo* subculture as a multidimensional practice with crime being just one component that is sometimes utilized by a small group of youngsters. Schools and police, however, have a fixed understanding of *cholo*. This subculture is about attitudes, choice of style, and a temporarily enacted performance, and, thus, it is a very fluid label that can be deployed and retracted based on those choices on any given day. A youngster could dress *cholo* one day and then business casual for work the next, without stigma—at least not until schools and police translate *cholo* as "gang member." Law enforcement is immensely powerful in defining *cholo* subculture as criminal. Schools and other community members are heavily influenced by police labels and discourses and respond by treating young people as criminal threats—with suspicion, harsh discipline, and calls to police.

Thus, through this collective social process, institutions and their agents—from police, whom we expect to be punitive, to parents, whom we might not—impose a fixed and stagnant identity on the otherwise fluid style expressions of youths placed at risk. I refer to this as cultural misframing. Cultural misframing is the process by which institutions construct, define, and impose simplistic, fixed, negative identities on individuals based on misunderstandings of their symbols, language, expressions, and actions. Conventional institutions often misunderstand marginalized individual's cultural frames. They, in turn, impose labels on these individuals that redefine their intentions, actions, and thoughts. This cultural misframing leads to dire consequences. Once again, these youths become human targets, menacing or disreputable individuals who require punishment. Therefore, *cholo* is a youth subculture like many others—punk, jock, surfer, skater, hipster—but when it is criminalized by law enforcement, other institutions and authorities are given carte blanche to dole out discipline and punishment. Once they are treated as outcasts, youths seek ways to restore their dignity and resist a system they perceive as repressive.

Cholo style in Riverland stemmed from the youths' deep-rooted desire to transform their social conditions and resist discriminatory treatment. When they adopted *cholo* style, youths took ownership of their difference, making it something they created. They could control how they were identified and differentiate themselves from the privileged class they were expected to aspire to, but were obstructed from joining. Flaco, a nineteen-year-old gang-associated youth explained:

> If I grow my hair out then I'ma conform. Why do I want to do something they want me to do? I want them to accept me for me.

As individuals who encounter "multiple marginalization"—economic, social, interpersonal—youth in barrio gangs experience some of the most extreme consequences of inequality (Vigil 1988; Durán 2013). In Riverland, youths were caught between two cultures and marginalized in both, too far removed from one and not yet accepted by the other (see Martínez 1998). Youth often join neighborhood cliques to resist the racial and economic subordination that leaves their communities vulnerable to exploitation (Jankowski 1991). Street groups offer, not only some support for youth in the barrio, but also the cultural empowerment that comes from being able to reject a society that rejects them. Subculture theory in criminology argues that some individuals living in poverty will develop deviant subcultures and commit crime as a means to resist and reject a mainstream system that has rejected them (Lemert 1951; Becker 1963).

But beyond rejecting their rejecters, even the most disreputable gang-associated young people reported a deep desire for acceptance, recognition, and incorporation into conventional society. They imagined themselves in a nine-to-five job, with a high school diploma or even a college degree. In all interviews, I asked the boys, "What would it take to get you off the streets, to stop you from being arrested again?" A fifteen-year-old's response spoke for most: "Shit! A job! Pay me twelve dollars an hour and I'll even wear skinny jeans, homie!"

Such a statement lays bare the intractable links between the lack of socioeconomic opportunity and the multiple cultural frames these youths are forced to navigate, each tied to a set of institutions in which these young people struggle, and usually fail, to be recognized and respected. So while these Riverland youths would not conform to an exploitable labor status and stigma, they would accept viable opportunities.

The problem lies not in a stubborn identity these boys have adopted whose foundational pillar is to oppose conventional values and practices, but rather, the boys' multiple and conflicting identities: One advises the boys to reject the system because it has rejected them; another demands they prove their worth through working and going to school; and yet another nudges them toward prison to reach the next level of "hardness." In a proverbial Cherokee story, a grandfather tells his grandson that there are two wolves within all humans: one filled with love and compassion, and another filled with fear and anger.

The grandson asks, "Which one wins, grandfather"?

The grandfather responds, "It is the one that you feed."

Similarly, gang-associated youth are dealt multiple frames: some conventional, others deviant and delinquent. The frames that are "fed" more support, more resources, and more affirmation from community institutions are those that resonate most with the boys. The boys who adopted a gangster style did so because those frames received the strongest positive support within their local context. For them, conventional culture—white, middle-class values, styles, frames, and tastes—were associated too often with negative interactions with authority figures, which reduced their influence. Time after time, teachers or police officers failed to demonstrate a belief that gang-associated youths could follow conventional frames, a lack of faith that deflated the youths' sense of belonging and association with such norms. Instead, they turned away to align deliberately and forcibly with the more accepting subculture. Their positive interactions with peers who understood their experiences strengthened those subcultural scripts that rejected conventional norms.

In separating themselves, gang-associated youths developed their own cultural performances and used unique stylistic appropriations to mark their difference. They commonly wore oversized work pants and large white or blue T-shirts. A few regularly wore Dodgers or Cowboys jerseys, which corresponded with the blue themes common among *Sureno* street cliques, gangs that have symbolic or real affiliation to the Mexican Mafia prison gang. Whether closely networked to the mafia or simply autonomous adopters of *Sureno* style, the youth who dressed that way donned a label signifying "gang" to other youth and to authorities. Other youths wore black T-shirts or hoodies saying "Riverland" or "South Side." Few ever wore conventional brand names or logos, like Nike or Hurley. Many wore white sneakers kept impeccably clean, and their hair was always either shaved or cropped to about half an inch or less.

Tito illustrates *cholo* style. When I first met him, he was wearing khaki-colored work pants, several sizes too big, pulled up high around his belly and fastened with a black belt. Over his large white T-shirt that hung loose to his mid-thigh, he layered another shirt, which made him look bulkier than he actually was. His head was shaved, and he had letters representing his neighborhood tattooed on his forearms.

Thirty-four of the initial fifty-seven gang-associated youths in our focus groups had tattoos, which embodied a style that they could call their own, outside the norm. A few went beyond this stylistic explanation and referred to a tattoo as a means of resisting mainstream expectations—a "symbolic challenge to the overt and indirect forms of domination," according to cultural theorist Ben Olguin (1997) who argues that the Latino male body has become a central battlefield in the war on crime, where alleged gang members become hyper-policed:

> The "adorned" body of the collective and individual "Hispanic male subject" is read and also written on by a variety of narrators—police officers, prosecutors, and judges, as well as prison administrators, guards, and even prisoners themselves. These interventions help

transform the body into a network of signifiers that at once affirm the "suspected" and/or "convicted criminal's" personal identity while simultaneously confirming his abject status in society. (161)

In this struggle, these Latino males reclaim their bodies by inscribing their own meanings, performance, and resistance onto themselves. Olguin describes the act of tattooing as "the Latino (*lumpenproletariat*) practice of ritually marking a space for the purpose of laying a symbolic and even material claim on it" (162). This reclamation of the body from a punitive landscape is infused with gang and barrio references, as well as religious, cultural, and family images. Among the Riverland boys, tattoos included images of the Virgin Mary, *La Virgen de Guadalupe*, Jesus Christ, Aztec symbols, the word "Riverland," and family names.

The youths understood that appropriating a *cholo* identity marked them for persecution and police attention because in the public sphere they stood out as a counterpoint to the safe-city image that Riverland worked hard to project. Tito elaborates:

> Those fools will tell us to get the fuck out of here 'cause they don't want the tourists to be—or the yeah—the tourists and the white people to get scared.

Nevertheless, they remained steadfast in their stylistic stance because their visible opposition appeared to be the entire point.

Although not inherently deviant, *cholo* style is intentionally oppositional to the mainstream (Vigil 1988), and, understandably, *cholo* subculture has an appeal much broader than gang-involved youth. This culture of resistance, and its associated styles and performance, resonates with many unaffiliated barrio youth because it speaks to struggles that affect the entire community. For example, fifteen-year-old Ricardo, who reported not being in the gang and did not plan to join, dressed in baggy pants and occasionally shaved his head. Asked if he thought his appearance might make others believe he was a gang-associated youth, he said,

Yeah, but this is what I like to wear. I don't care what they think. They still gotta respect me. Just 'cause I don't want to be in the gang doesn't mean I don't like being gangster.

Youth clearly made this differentiation between being gang members or simply *cholo*, a generic style, and being a bona fide gang member or affiliated with an alleged criminal enterprise.

According to historian Robin Kelley (1997), the gangster appeals to youth as a response to socioeconomic subjugation and as a challenge to authority in general, one in which the marginalized are imagined as all-powerful. Similarly, Stuart Cosgrove (1984) noted that the *pachucos* (Mexican American zoot-suit-wearing youths) of the 1940s adopted a style of dress to contest their social invisibility. To those who wore them, zoot suits were "a spectacular reminder that the social order had failed to contain their energy and difference . . . a subcultural gesture that refused to concede to the manners of subservience" (Cosgrove 1984, 78). Segregated from mainstream society and, therefore, alienated from the ambitions of their immigrant parents, the *pachucos* rebelled by flaunting their difference. In the process, they developed a culture that critiqued racism and the unequal American class structure.

Both *pachuco* and *cholo* styles "became cultural productions signifying unique forms of resistance by youth of color against the dominant image of style and culture embraced by other young people of these eras" (Bejarano 2005, 90). In accentuating difference, youth subcultures empower what society has devalued, making their styles attractive to marginalized youth. In a way, adopting an alternative style became somewhat of an informal social movement in which marginalized youth could portray their culture through dress and appearance. But even these representations of resistance are not fixed; youths engage them selectively, based on interactions with power.

Sociologist Erving Goffman posited that individuals construct the impressions they make on others in social settings to create perceptions they want others to have of them. In his dramaturgical theory, Goffman (1959) compared social interactions to a theatrical play. People constantly engage in "impression management" as they use the resources around them to develop the most ideal impression of themselves. We use aspects of social interactions to convey individual identities through specific forms of dress (Garot and Katz 2003; Entwhistle 2001), language (Widdicombe and Wooffitt 1995), and mannerisms (Sudnow 1978). Whether the black leather jackets of the 1950s, the punk styles of the 1970s, or the rap and hip-hop styles of the 1990s, individuals use aspects of daily self-presentation to place themselves within specific cultural contexts and categories, reflecting particularities of their identity, such as class (MacLeod 2008), sexuality (Yoshino 2006), and race (Wieder and Pratt 1989). Among the South Riverland youths, "impression management" centered on demanding dignity, with their impeccably clean clothes and sneakers emblematic of that stance.

Gang association for the Riverland boys became a performed identity that defied mainstream values and the criminalization of their community in that it provided a platform from which they could distinguish themselves from authority figures' expectations (Garot 2010; Durán 2013; Mendoza-Denton 2008). *Cholo* style was a tool in this performed identity, and because it projected the image of a Latino challenging the mainstream cultural values, it held an importance far deeper than belonging to a specific neighborhood or clique. Many youths expressed feeling uncomfortable in clothes they claimed were for white people and could never imagine giving up their chosen style—unless they found a viable, well-paying job. In that case, performing mainstream respectability for a white, middle-class audience was understood as the price to be paid for a regular, sustainable paycheck. Otherwise, the youths were adamant in their attachment to *cholo* style regardless of the associated risks. As eighteen-year-old Santos said, "I'm not gonna change my style just for a stupid ass cop that thinks I'm gonna, you know, get into something."

In addition to attached messages of resistance to mainstream values and marginalization, *cholo* style was simply a practical approach to life in poverty conditions. In a focus group, a pair of boys reminded us that most of the clothing—white T-shirts, baggy jeans, NFL wear—became popular *cholo* fashions because they were readily available for poor urban youth:

> JUAN: Why does it matter what we're wearing in the first place? The cops are always giving us shit, like we're wearing a uniform, they say that we're wearing a uniform 'cause we're wearing Dickies! Well they're cheap. What little we have, we're gonna go buy a fuckin'...
>
> JASON: ... go buy some Dockers and what not.

Unlike the mainstream fashions, presumably more acceptable to authority figures, white T-shirts and Dickies pants were inexpensive and durable, and a shaved head required only clippers and a razor that could be reused several times, as opposed to a monthly fifteen- to twenty-dollar barbershop haircut.

Because the boys' appearance contradicted the dominant image of Riverland as a profitable, carefree resort town, these youths were harassed by police and kept away from any public events expected to draw large crowds and considerable commercial revenue. Many were picked up before holiday or city celebrations and detained for the duration without charges or with bogus charges; others reported being arrested on sight should they try to attend such public events. For example, about two weeks prior to the town's famous yearly parade days, many boys informed me they might not be around for interviews or observations because, as Tito explained:

> They start violating us [arrest for violating terms of probation] around this time. They find stupid excuses for arresting us like a few days before the parade days, dog. They just take us in and we're stuck there for the weekend. Monday we have court and get released. After all the partying is over.

Riverland depended on a docile servant community (of color), available to cater to the whims of this privileged population, but by adopting *cholo* styles that magnified their visibility in the public sphere, marginalized youth challenged this power and authority— and paid the consequences. Nonetheless, the feeling of dignity and affirmation often outweighed the punitive consequences meted out by the state. In this sense, punishment is not always a deterrent to crime, especially if that crime is committed for purposes related to feelings of redemption or dignity enhancement (see Braithwaite 1989).

Frames as a Source of Empowerment

Devalued in mainstream society along race and class hierarchies, Latino youths created street cultures to promote their own self-worth (Rodriguez 2005). In creating their own culture, these youths established their own styles and identities in which to find value instead of adopting cultural norms that constantly reminded them they did not belong. Within this street-oriented, working-class Latino culture, they crafted for themselves a spot in the center, not at the margins. Although the youth culture was resistance, it was not necessarily oppositional. In other words, young people may have rejected their rejecters, but they simultaneously hankered to gain acceptance in the mainstream, to hold well-paying, steady jobs, and to further their education. Even as these youths were adept at working within the cultural frame of *cholo* and the street life it stylized, their proficiency within this frame would not help them accomplish social mobility—and they knew it. This illustrates how young people are cognizant and rational about the frames at their disposal. While they choose street-life-oriented cultural frames, they are aware of others, like a college-going student or the employed, reformed O.G. (original gangster).

They may have had other choices, but these choices had limited resources in the everyday, real world of South Riverland. On any given day, if a young person chose to make a change for the better, to dream about educational and occupational success, the help available to make this dream come true was scarce in the neighborhood and from authority figures. For example, many youths defaulted to street life only after suffering rejection from multiple institutions—family, schools, police, and the labor market. Thus, negative interactions with authority figures weakened the cultural frames of success in school and work and strengthened those of the gang and street life. Institutions play a powerful role in determining which cultural frames young people gravitate toward and are able to utilize.

Sánchez-Jankowski (1991) theorizes that teenagers join street gangs as a youthful, temporary rebellion against the marginal economic futures that await them in adulthood. However, John Hagedorn (1988) argues that in the postindustrial economy, this temporary rebellion finds more permanence as working-class youths encounter greater difficulty finding stable employment. Based on these ideas, the South Riverland youths' adoption of highly visible *cholo* styles could indicate resistance to the mainstream expectation that they become servants of privileged whites. Conscious of the few opportunities to find legitimate career paths, Latino youth adopted appearances they knew would block them from the low-level service positions they were expected to fill. They tapped into racist fears of their inherent criminality to create a public impression that would counter the image of the submissive, stigmatized servant. In a racialized, hyperexploited service economy, these youths deliberately put themselves out of service to retain their dignity. They changed the meaning of race by pushing back against a system that had constructed their "Mexican" parents as a cheap labor force. Instead, they now participated in the construction of "Mexican" as rebellious and resistant, even if this meant encountering the wrath of the punitive state. In this sense, the cultural frames that young people were able to choose and utilize became part of a racial formation process (see Bonilla-Silva 2006 and Omi and Winant 1994).

Luis, a seventeen-year-old gang-associated youth who wore forty-eight-inch pants on his thirty-four-inch waist, described the effect of his appearance: "I feel like when I dress like this, and like the way

I look and everything, it gives me like power. Like I feel like, more like in control and all that." One of his friends suggested the feeling was based on being able to scare people. Luis replied, "Yeah, like I could! . . . I don't think like 'Oh, people look at me bad,' I think of people like they're scared." By marking himself as a person the mainstream public should fear, Luis forced people to respect him as a threat, and thus he could claim power. In this sense, these youths preferred to be feared rather than to be stigmatized, marginalized, and exploited as servants to a privileged white class.

Cholo style, despite its relatively minimalist fashions, demands attention and contests social invisibility because it taps persistent racist assumptions of the inherent danger Latinos pose to public safety. The hype of the gang threat magnifies public fears of youth of color and makes street styles all the more noticeable. Regardless of actual migration status or country of origin, stereotypes of violent Mexicans are wielded against all Latinos in the United States, challenging their citizenship rights and keeping migrants deportable, and thus, economically exploitable (DeGenova 2002; Ngai 2014; Chavez 2008; Newton 2008). Perceptions of Mexican illegality extend this vulnerability to the Latino community at large (Barrera 1979; Acuña 2004; Newton 2008; Ngai 2014), although much can be mediated through various forms of status and cultural capital. Facing daily reminders of their marginality and relative inability to combat the structures working against them, the South Riverland boys played on mainstream racist fears to retain some power in the public sphere. *Cholo* or thug cultural frames remained vigorous in the lives of these marginalized young people precisely because they offered practical, problem-solving solutions to the dilemmas of everyday life: Where do I belong? How do I deal with my emotions? How do I nourish myself? Whose got my back?

The Strength of Weak Frames

Cholo performance is rarely absolute, but occurs across a continuum of implementation, depending on personal needs and desires. Police

evaluate the intensity of a youth's *cholo* style and assign the individual a corresponding degree of criminality (Miller 1995). With
that knowledge, youths recognize they will encounter greater levels
of criminalization and violence with more intense displays of *cholo*
identity.

Chuy, a seventeen-year-old gang-associated youth, explained why
he stopped shaving his head after wearing it in this style for four
years: "[A bald head] causes too much attraction. So . . . let it grow
out a little bit you know?" However, to Chuy, growing his hair meant
adopting a fade style, about a quarter inch in length, and he still wore
baggy pants and plaid Pendleton shirts. He did not abandon his performance, but modified its intensity after his shaved head caused
too many problems. Despite this, people still saw him as a threat.
Taking steps to be less intensely *cholo* did not necessarily translate
into decriminalization of these youths in the view of the institutions
they frequented. Criminal labels are like radioactive waste: They actively linger indefinitely into the future. The artifacts these labels
leave behind include gang databases, criminal records, gang injunctions, gang enhancements, and corresponding exclusion from
schools and the labor market.

Some youths also recognized a need to balance this self-
presentation with those more acceptable in mainstream society.
They knew that drastic or permanent displays of *cholo* identity could
bar them from the limited opportunities they might really need, despite their reluctance to take them. For instance, most of the youths
had tattoos, but they tended to be on their chests, stomachs, backs,
or upper arms where they could be more easily covered. Few had tattoos on their necks or faces, a more extreme display of gang association and refusal to conform to conventional standards, including
employment in service positions. Even Luis, who valued the fear he
could instill in strangers, recognized he could embody this performance only when he was not working at his job as a busboy in a high-
end restaurant, deferring to wealthy patrons. Off the clock, he could
adopt his more fearsome identity and regain the empowerment that
he sacrificed on the job. The youths resisted their positioning in the

local labor market, but most could not afford to reject it entirely. They did not solely practice a culture of resistance or a resistance subculture; much of the time they also sought conventional avenues for becoming adults, because even weak cultural frames have a lot of strength.

The cultural frames that constituted messages, ideas, perceptions, interactions, and symbols nudging young people to stay legit, get and keep a job, go to school, and stay away from the gang remained weak in South Riverland because they were resource deprived. The job market was weak and wages low; role models were few; and schools and police misframed young people's cultures. If such resources were stronger, they could fortify young people's desires, aspirations, and actions to incorporate into the conventional world. Nevertheless, these weak frames still resonated strongly in the minds and thoughts of marginalized young people, and even the slightest opportunity, like a job lead or a positive connection with a teacher, propagated these weak frames, making them stronger within short spans of time, facilitating a process of model shifting.

Conventional frames are not only present in the lives of marginalized young people, but they can be fortified with the help of positive interactions with authority figures and with viable jobs or culturally relevant educational programs. Take, for example, Mark, the student at Punta Vista School who was labeled "angry" and who displayed a hypermasculine attitude on the streets, starting fights or threatening to beat or kill people every time I saw him. Fourteen months into my observations, Mark's persistent behavior landed him in juvenile hall for assault and then for violating probation. One day, he returned from being locked up for two weeks and asked if I knew about any available jobs. I asked what sort of work he wanted. "A sushi chef," he said. "I want to be a sushi chef. Cut up some fish and what not." I helped him write a resume with that objective, and a few weeks later Mark landed a job, not as a sushi chef, but as a dishwasher at a sushi restaurant. Over two months, he maintained that job and was promoted to waiter. I went to eat at his restaurant to pay him a visit.

Mark has a gleaming smile and it doesn't feel fake like a customer service friendly smile but genuine. As he later explains to me, "I'm happy 'cause I got a job and I am happy you get to see me doing it." He looks relaxed, poised, and with a purpose. He wears loose-fitting black dress slacks, black dress shoes, a white dress shirt, and skinny black tie. He approaches the table with a huge smile, appearing proud and ready to impress. "Rios, sir, how can I help you?" sounding very official. He looks down at his notepad and stares back at me.

"Let me get a . . . what's good here, man?"

"You should try the volcano rolls. They are made with salmon, toasted sesame seeds, Ikura, and topped with shrimp tempura."

"Ikura! What's Ikura, man?" I ask.

"Oh, salmon eggs, it's salmon eggs, Rios . . . and don't forget to order some spicy edamame. It's got a great taste."

I order the volcano roll, edamame, and miso soup. Mark moves about tending to other tables. Despite only being on the job [as a waiter] for a few weeks, he is on it. He looks like a professional; no one would guess that just a few weeks ago he was out on the streets putting in work or at school being labeled an at-risk angry student. He does have a tattoo on his hand with three letters each about one inch tall, representing his gang "SST." I ask him what he tells his boss and customers about it. He replies, "I tell them it was a social club that I was part of when I was a kid and that I found a home there when I really needed one. . . . They tell me, 'Oh, like Boys and Girls Club?' I say yeah, just like that."

Mark represents one of the young people who have been criminalized in poor neighborhoods but have been able to draw upon their grit to avoid further incarceration—someone whose model shifting paid off. Some young people encounter opportunities and seize them to improve their social conditions. These opportunities, like employment, reinforce those cultural frames that call on individuals to prove themselves through productive activities, earning a decent living, attending school, and striving for a professional career. These frames are not difficult to bring out among marginalized young people and can be readily deployed under the right conditions, including the youth's desire to change, positive interactions with authority figures, and employment and educational opportunities. But in reality, young people in South Riverland and many marginalized communities are continually policed and treated as suspects and risks. Once a label has been created and imposed, the system's ability to facilitate model shifting—or the ability to encounter and utilize multiple frames—is diminished. When schools and police label a problem as a "problem," they tend to treat this problem with tunnel vision, targeting it with simplistic, in this case, punitive solutions that perpetuate negative interactions. As a result, these negative interactions spur youths to adopt frames that can lead to negative outcomes.

Amplified Criminalization and the Tragedy of Performance

Some youths who appropriate the fashions of specific subcultures can come to adopt the group's criminalized status as well. Identifying with criminalized street culture invites condemnation and underscores the alienation that perhaps these youths already feel. Scores of gang-associated youths adopt *cholo* styles, apparently because to be feared is better than to be invisible (Anderson 1999; Dance 2005). But as they adopt *cholo* identities, youths frequently become indistinguishable from criminal gang members in the eyes of authority figures, who, in turn, falsely inflate the threat of street groups and associate youth of color in specific contexts with violent street crime. In past anti-gang sweeps, police have detained teenagers for wearing red shoelaces or exchanging complex handshakes (Davis 1999), behavior that is now enough to be placed on California's gang database (Parenti 2000; Rios 2011).

Tito explained a scenario of police surveillance and harassment he experienced:

> One time I was in front of [a liquor store] and the cops would say like you don't have to hang around with those losers. They are nobody. This guy was drinking a beer and they like got the beer and poured it out and said this is for your dead homies. That is very disrespectful. The cops would usually get off the car or if not just park somewhere and just watch us. I got kind of used to it already. But it does get on my nerves because we are just outside and they have to be looking at us all the time.

By mocking the youth's cultural symbolism, in this case a ritual of paying homage to dead loved ones by pouring a sip of one's drink on the ground, police created yet another layer of social distance. Humiliation, disrespect, and a deep sense of resentment followed these kinds of actions, creating a deeper bond between youths who collectively experienced this perceived injustice.

Much of the general public also has adopted this criminalization of youth of color, which affects interactions with other adults in the community. Ricardo shared this story of criminalization:

> There was this lady that lives down the street. . . . Me and two other homies were walking by, and she's *gringa* [white]. Then I walked past her and she just dogs us. She's like "I'll go inside." . . . One night the narcs [gang unit police officers] had went by and she told her husband, "Don't worry, the cops are here, they'll get him."

Economic Context

Despite the stigma and risks, none of the boys were willing to switch to an appearance they knew authorities preferred, simply to comply with some social assumption. The only factor that could change their appearance was the promise of well-paying employment:

TITO: Set me up with an interview I'd be there, get a pair of tighter
pants—shit homes, I'll get rid of my baggy clothes.

V.R.: You would change the way you dress for sixteen, twenty dollars
an hour?

TITO: Hell yeah! Once they paid me I'd wear some more Levis, some
Dockers. I'll even wear some tight pants!

This willingness to alter their appearance for economic opportunities indicated that the street styles were a malleable form of resistance against the marginal roles the local labor market typically
offered them. If they could access better economic opportunities,
they were willing to frame switch and learn new interaction skills
and performances. Despite the marginalization they suffered, they
didn't refuse to participate in mainstream society, but only in the
subservient positions to which they were relegated. While a response
to deep-seated race, class, and gender dynamics, their performance
was pliable and shifted as cultural and material resources became
available (or were denied). But because employment that they considered as dignified was typically unavailable, they adopted appearances they knew would block them from being hired for the marginal positions they did not want. Santos described this dilemma:
"You can't just show up all bald-headed and be all 'homie, where's
my application?' I'm growing my hair out to try to get a job. I tried it
once but it didn't work so I just shaved my shit again."

Unstable living conditions and failing to find economic opportunities can quickly lead young people down a detrimental path.
Flaco's story is a case in point. The last time I saw Flaco, I helped
him develop his resume so he could seek a job to help his "lady"
with her two kids. Later I learned his family had experienced two
job losses in the economic downturn: Flaco's stepfather and older
brother, who had been paying the mortgage on their four-bedroom
house, both lost their jobs. The bank had foreclosed on their home,
and the family moved to a studio apartment where Flaco, his sister,
and brother slept on the floor next to their mother and stepfather's
bed. Then Flaco's stepfather asked him to move out. Flaco could not

afford to live in Riverland, so he moved to South Los Angeles to live with relatives. A few days later, he committed suicide by hanging himself. Flaco's death illustrates how the lack of economic opportunities renders these young people vulnerable.

Expected to assume subservient roles within Riverland's social hierarchy and labor market, local Latinos were stigmatized from a young age. But by becoming *cholos*, these youths found a way to publicly resist this degrading marginality. *Cholo* performance provided a way to reject the social systems that had rejected them. Who can mark you, if you first mark yourself? This self-imposed deviation from a "normal" aesthetic provided *cholos* with control over their identities and empowerment within the public sphere. By playing to mainstream fears of nonwhite criminality, young Latinos dramatized their difference and, thereby, contested their social invisibility.

But the risks and challenges of adopting *cholo* styles are great. *Cholos* are commonly registered in gang databases that are used to assign enhancements and injunctions that mandate prison time. Repeated arrests and prolonged prison terms further limit already marginal employment opportunities (Pager 2007) and detrimentally affect inmates' families (Comfort 2008). Life on the streets and in correctional facilities enables drug and alcohol abuse, and few treatment options are available to these individuals. Many end up incarcerated, permanently injured, or dead, and almost all acquire negative credentials that permanently mark them as unemployable and irredeemable. In addition, *cholo* performance can have a dangerous impact on young women in the community, as young men develop a perilous masculinity that reinforces female subjugation. In this study, I found that these youngsters had immense cultural heterogeneity. Their ability to switch identities or model shift allowed them to take advantage of the few opportunities available to them. However, when these opportunities were lacking, their adaptation of harmful frames became pronounced.

Masculinity

A negative consequence of not having enough resources to reinforce favorable notions of masculinity—like a hard-work ethic, respect for women, and engaging in one's community—was the development of a perilous masculinity. Many youths displayed negative attitudes toward young women in their lives, regularly referring to them as "bitches," and using phrases like "slap a bitch" to discuss reprimanding others—male or female—who did not respect them. To display resistance to the subordination they faced in society, these young Latinos adopted tough, violent, and defiant personae. They then projected this performance onto young women, as a patriarchal cultural frame became one available avenue to empowerment.

For most of the boys, two of the main milestones in achieving manhood were having sex and getting arrested. Youths who had frequent sex or had been arrested multiple times were afforded greater respect. Whether the young men committed crimes to acquire money, to gain status among peers, or to resist their marginalization, their personal vendettas almost always affected the young women around them. The young males' resistance to marginalization was often at the expense of the young women, since to many young men resistance meant claiming their manhood in more assertive ways. As they sought pride, dignity, and defiance of subservience, their identities became more masculinized, less self-consciously performed, and they were more demeaning and brutal toward young women. The more *cholos* resisted marginalization, the more any identity deemed "feminine" even in the narrowest of terms was vulnerable to their aggression.

This perilous masculinity did not develop in a vacuum within Latino street culture, but through interactions with educational, criminal justice, and community institutions that inculcated a defensive male performance (see Rios 2009). Domination is frequently inflicted through the axis of race, class, or gender, and, as these boys resisted one or two of these axes, they sometimes perpetuated oppression on the remaining one. Although these young men did not see themselves as performing resistance, they tried to become what they performed. In doing so, they came to hate any differences that threatened their identity performance as stable, solid, and real. The following chapter examines in depth, through a cultural framing perspective, how masculinity operates in the lives of Riverland youths.

CHAPTER FOUR

Multiple Manhoods

(with Rachel Sarabia)

When I first met Jason, he was twenty years old with a criminal record and considered himself an "active gang member."[1] Jason garnered respect from his "homies" because he had spent much of his teenage years "putting in work" on the streets, which meant fighting, dealing drugs, and stealing. Jason explained:

> Well, you have to earn respect. Nobody gives it to you. If you give respect to the right people, you get respect from the right people . . . you hold your ground you know, just throw down [fight]. . . . Like some fool tries make you look like a bitch, then you throw down [fight] and that's how they look at respect you know?

In my observations, I saw Jason "calling shots" in the neighborhood, giving orders to other young men, and avoiding victimization and incarceration by having other young men look out for him when conflict arose. But I also noticed that Jason was one of the few active gang members who escaped police searches and harassment.

One day, I was standing in front of Golden State Liquors with six boys, four of whom were drinking tall cans of Arizona Iced Tea. A Gang Suppression Team member—police officers responsible for monitoring gang members—pulled up to the curb, stepped out of his vehicle, and asked, "What are you drinking?" Most of the boys ignored him; two shrugged their shoulders. The officer signaled Julio to come closer, but Julio ignored him.

"If you don't come here," the officer warned, "I'm gonna make you look really bad in front of your homies."

Julio walked over, and the officer grabbed him by the shirt, pressuring him to sit on the curb. Then, he lifted Julio up by the shirt and emptied his pockets. Using his radio, the officer checked if Julio had a police record or any outstanding warrants. He proceeded to do the same for all the others—except for Jason.

Before driving off, the officer looked at Jason and said, "I'll see you at the bagel shop. . . . Tell these boys they need to get a job like you."

Jason worked at a local bagel shop where police officers who patrolled the neighborhood often stopped, which is why he believed the police gave him more respect than some of the other young men. "Police know I am a hard worker," he said. "That's what they expect of me. I'm a family man and I don't commit crime anymore." Among more than eighty young men I encountered during my five-year study, Jason was one of only six homies who held a steady full-time job.

Jason often brought his four-year-old son, Junior, with him to hang out at the park or in front of the liquor store. Junior wore a blue bandana in his rear pocket, a sign representing the Mexican Mafia, and sometimes Jason urged him to play-fight with older neighborhood kids. He said he wanted Junior to learn to be a man, which entailed learning about street life, how to protect himself, and how to demand respect.

Although Jason believed that gang parents and older gang members sometimes played a negative role in the life of their younger kin, he did not realize that his own actions to socialize his son to be a tough man might also have a negative impact:

> It's like the families and older guys force them to join [the gang]. It's like a circle that can offer protection . . . well, not just force them, but also they don't have the money to buy this and that, so people join gangs for protection and go rob and shit. But my son, I don't want him doing all that nutty stuff.

Jason was an active father who wanted his son to have a bright future. Frequently, he could be seen pushing his son in a stroller through the neighborhood and tending to his needs. Yet, he did not as often consider how the actions and lessons of manhood performed around his boy might encourage Junior to join a gang in the future. To Jason, Junior was partaking in "child's play."

Jason always appeared incredibly loyal and respectful to his girlfriend, even on the street where other young women were called "bitches" and "hos" by their partners or other boys and could be physically or symbolically attacked. Jason had developed the ability to balance various manifestations of masculinity, which yielded diverse benefits: respect on the streets, acknowledgment from police, a healthy romantic relationship, and the reputation as a "manly son."

However, Jason's experience was unusual. Although all of the young men in this study adopted different forms of masculinity, Jason was one of the few who experienced associated positive outcomes. More commonly, young men displayed their masculinity in a way that resulted in their arrest for challenging or assaulting police officers and others. A comparison of Jason's experience with that of other young men yielded concrete examples of the various practices of masculinity in this South Riverland neighborhood.

These gang-associated young men used masculinity as a central vehicle by which to compensate for race and class subordination. In an effort to maintain dignity and respect, they used differing forms of masculinity (subordinate, street, working class, dominant, and hyper) at various times, a process we refer to as synthesized masculinities. The young men we studied synthesized masculinities to acquire social status and to contest various forms of subordination. Like other forms of gender and sexuality practice, the masculinities they practiced were fluid, situated, and shifting.

In addition to the morals and values of manhood the young men learned from being on the streets, they also found masculinity within criminalization—specifically, negative encounters with school, police, juvenile hall, and probation authorities. One consequence of criminalization and punitive social control for these boys was the development of a specific set of gendered practices that obstructed desistance from crime, positive social relationships, and social mobility. By analyzing the perceptions and actions of these young men, we uncovered how masculinity emerged from and reflected race, class, and gender subordination. Jason's discussion of "being a man" represented how many of the boys developed synthesized masculinities, a strategic and situational display of various masculinities. Various frames representing masculinity were meshed together to embody a masculinity that allowed the boys to feel empowered in multiple settings.

Like Jason, many of the other boys relied on masculinity to obtain respect and cope with race and class marginality; however, their approaches often led instead to victimization, stigmatization, and incarceration. With limited access to traditional pathways to accomplish conventional masculinity—that ideal in which a man works hard, makes good money, and supports his family—the boys sought alternative ways to achieve manhood. Synthesized masculinities allowed these young men to creatively accomplish masculinity throughout their lives in their effort to access resources they perceived to be lacking and to compensate for other forms of domination.

Masculinities

Researchers who study masculinity examine the ways that "different ideologies about manhood develop, change, [and] are combined, amended and contested" (Bederman 1996). Masculinity is dynamic, constructed, and realized through interactions with others (Carrigan, Connell, and Lee 1985; Kimmel 2003). Kimmel (2003) argues that manhood is accomplished through cultural symbols and the subordination of women. Among American men, achieving masculinity is a "relentless test," and failure to embody, affirm, or accomplish it is a "source of men's confusion and pain" (Kimmel 2003, 58). But masculinities are also "subject positions taken up by different men in different cultural contexts" (Cooper 2009, 685). Because masculinity is always intersecting with sexuality, race, and class, a plurality of masculine identities exists rather than one single identity (Carrigan et al. 1985; Connell 1991).

Connell proposed the notion of "hegemonic masculinity" as the dominant form of masculinity in a hierarchy of masculinities and amid a constant struggle for dominance (Connell and Messerschmidt 2005). Hegemonic masculinity describes practices by which privileged males dominate women and other marginalized men as they seek to produce wealth, achieve recognition from mainstream institutions, and demonstrate a respectable patriarchal persona. Accomplishing this sort of masculinity is almost impossible for less affluent, marginalized men because of the relentless demands, not only to acquire wealth, but also to portray a certain white male aesthetic (e.g., Carter 2003; Lopez 2002; Rios 2009). Thus, working-class, nonwhite, or gay men may seek other avenues to achieve manhood. As Adams and Savran (2002) argue, all men attempt to accomplish masculinity, but not all men desire the same type of masculinity, nor do they accomplish it at the same rate or with the same ease. Those unable to demonstrate the same markers of masculinity as privileged men may seek "compensatory masculinities" (e.g., Pyke 1996), through other—often deviant—behaviors, such as drug and alcohol use/abuse, sexual carousing, and brawling, to illustrate their resistance to and independence from existing power structures (Pyke 1996). Toughness, dominance, and the willingness to resort to violence to resolve interpersonal conflicts are central resources for men less able to acquire the resources of mainstream masculinity (e.g., Anderson 1999; Harris 2000; Messerschmidt 1993; Rios 2009).

Not all marginalized men resort to compensatory masculinity, however, but instead embrace more conventional but fluid forms that are "synthesized," depending heavily on context and type of interaction (peer-peer, male-female, youth–authority figure). Working-class masculinity, hypermasculinity, and street masculinity are, not only compensatory behaviors, but also components of fluid cultural frames that street-oriented young men draw upon as they navigate social contexts.

Beyond the dominant-subordinate dichotomy often discussed, we found a more complicated notion of dominant and subordinate masculinities that the young men synthesized through interactions with police in the neighborhood. These synthesized performances critically highlighted these youths' negotiation of street, working-class, dominant, and subordinate masculinities. These men were more than just "violent-prone individuals who mindlessly lash out at the world with hostility and aggression" (Young 2004). Rather, they were complex individuals negotiating barriers and creatively exploring opportunities in the world around them.

Law Enforcement, Masculinity Enforcement

A majority of the young men and women interviewed (forty-six of fifty-seven men, and fourteen of eighteen women) held negative worldviews about the police. All reported at least one negative interaction in which they felt victimized either through physical or verbal abuse. In my observations on the street and in ride-alongs with police, I observed a handful of positive interactions and many negative ones, although most interactions between youth and police were neutral. Often police simply questioned or cited the boys and let them go, but I witnessed times when police verbally degraded boys, used excessive force, and employed illegal searches. For many of the young men, the police represented one of many obstacles to their development and ability to find a place in the community. In their minds, the police, like others in society, grouped them as criminals and promoted that image to community members, potential employers, and school authorities. Through instilling fear of violence and incarceration, the police consistently tested, challenged, and degraded their masculinity. *emmasculation by police*

Policing is a male-dominated and masculine field (Cooper 2009; Dodsworth 2007; Harris 2000), and machismo has been central in police culture (Herbert 2006). Many of the police-youth encounters I witnessed involved masculinity challenges. Through exerting their dominance, police officers were "doing" gender (e.g., Martin 1999) as they strategically emasculated the youths to symbolically demonstrate the officers were the "real" men.

Clash between masculinity [handwritten margin note]

Police responded to perceived attacks on their masculine self-identity and authority with violence or threats of violence, an observation consistent with other research (Harris 2000). When they believed neighborhood youths were disrespecting them, they used threats or physical power to restore their dignity. Police officers got "macho" with youths, staging masculinity contests with them—contests rife with meaning in these young men's lives. The youths interpreted such actions as taunts, efforts to provoke the boys' anger so they would talk back or lash out and do something that would justify an arrest (Gau and Brunson 2010; Harris 2000; Sollund 2006).

Dreamy, a seventeen-year-old Latino male once arrested for possessing a marijuana pipe, represented many of the other boys' perceptions:

> Cops are a bunch of bullies. . . . They are always trying to act like they are bigger men than you. . . . They think we are organized crime or something, and, like, damn, we are just a bunch of homies that are kicking it. . . . I mean I think when you see a cop you should feel safe and you know kind of make you feel good, but hell no, when I see a cop I get fuckin' scared as hell! Even if I'm not doing anything wrong, I'm still fuckin' scared as hell!

Eighteen-year-old Angel, who had been arrested twice, once for a gang fight and once for violating probation, voiced similar interactions with police:

> They always say some fucked up shit to me. Once they told me, "Why don't you come work with us, *puta* [bitch]?" And sometimes they're like, "I promise I won't take you in if you do something for me [like giving them information on criminal activity]." *Pinche pen-*

dejos [fucking idiots]. It's all a trick. They are always on top of us. . . .
They're like "look, I know you're on probation," and they just keep
talking shit, talking shit. Cops don't respect us. They laugh at us. *En
serio* [seriously], they're just like, oh, look at these fools, they're just
a bunch of bitches.

Joker, a sixteen-year-old who hung out with the gang, but did well
in school and avoided fighting, drinking, and staying out late, related an incident when an officer used physical force on him:

The cops do nothing but harass. I go to school. I try to stay out of
trouble. Narc [undercover police] cars are always around. I see them
driving back and forth on my way to school. Sometimes I think I'm
just trippin'. It's like, fuck, why are they stopping here? You always
gotta look over your shoulder, dog, you know what I mean? They roll
up and they just stare at us. One time, they tried to stop me. I ran.
I bounced because it was curfew. I tried to hide. They found me. I
tried to tell them I got a fucked-up back, that I had been in a car
accident. I told them not to slam me. That fool grabbed me from the
neck, motherfucker, started cussing me out, fool. He fuckin' slams
the shit out of me dog, fuckin' scraped my face, my chin and shit.
And I'm just like, fuck, I got all dizzy. He was just talking shit. He
was mad. He was like, "Yeah I fucked you up, motherfucker, keep
running from me, you fuckin' little bitch. I'm gonna fuckin' bust you
this time." They always mistreating us.

One afternoon, four boys in this study were arrested in front of
a community center when three police officers arrived to disperse
a crowd of twenty suspected gang members loitering outside. Five
additional officers were called to provide backup. Jason started
taking pictures of the officers. The officers approached Jason and
started taking pictures of him with their cell phones. One officer got
so close, according to Jason, that he was hit in the face a few times
with the officer's phone. Jason pushed the officer's phone away. He
was arrested for attempted robbery, resisting an officer, battery on

a police officer, and participation in a criminal street gang. Three other boys were arrested for petty infractions.

Jason spent four months in jail for this incident. Tired of being photographed by police, he said he had decided to respond by taking a picture of the officers that day:

> Why can't we take pictures of them, but they can take them of us? It's a bunch of bullshit. They just slap a bunch of shit on us. They always try to put us in the wrong and make it look they are the innocent ones, the good guys.

The camera incident demonstrates the masculinity battles waged between officers and the boys. Police demanded respect, and when it was not given, they reacted quickly and harshly. According to the boys, police "create bogus charges": attempted robbery, resisting an officer, battery of a police officer, or participation in a criminal street gang in an attempt to control and entrap them.

Police consistently challenged and mocked the boys for their way of talking, their dress, their friends and associates, and their failure to display conventional masculinity. More than enforcing the law, police were enforcing masculinity out of a desire to preserve their authority, prove their manhood, and maintain their dominant status on the streets (Cooper 2009; Hahn 1971). The boys described officers as power-hungry individuals who had something to prove: that they were "manlier" than the gang. Criticizing police for overcompensating was an integral part of the boys' performances of masculinity. They believed they were the real men, and the police were weak individuals hiding behind badges and guns. But much of their manhood was constructed in direct response to power, in this case punitive police intervention in their lives.

Simultaneously, police attempted to reinforce a particular form of working-class masculinity that was less available to these particular young men than the officers seemed to understand. They pushed the idea that "a real man gets a job and provides for his family." Yet these boys' young age and poor education put them in the company of those with a 40 percent unemployment rate. If jobs existed, these boys were not among those getting hired.

Most of the officers serving the South Riverland community were white, and the boys viewed them as rich men with good jobs, even as they despised some of them. When officers gave advice to the boys, they used their profession as a reference point. "Right now you're just on probation for small stuff. You can still clean your record and become a cop one day," one officer told a group of four boys in front of the liquor store. Officers consistently made references to being "a real man" when they advised the boys. "Be a real man, get a job, leave the homies, go to school, and provide for your family," an officer told one boy as he stopped and searched him.

The boys understood the normative ideals for how to "become a man," even if they had yet to acquire the resources to do so. The following descriptions were representative:

A man is someone that can support their family . . . even with the struggle . . . having a job . . . putting support . . . having food on the table, a roof over their head, and clothes on their backs . . . that's a man. (Raul, 14)

Knowing how to work makes you a man. Being responsible. A man is somebody that, you know, doesn't back down. To be a man, you gotta be down for whatever. You stick around, or stick to what you say you're gonna do. You don't learn this stuff overnight though; becoming a man is a process. (Tito, 17)

I would want to be successful you know, and come back and help people that need it the most, like people that were . . . or kids that went through the same shit that I went through or something you know, just trying to give back to the community. . . . I mean hopefully college can help me figure that out, you know 'cause . . . a lot of people don't even know what they want to do you know, and when they go to college that's where they figure shit out. So that's what I'ma try to do. (Jose, 16)

Most boys believed gang life was just a stage in their development, and that one day, they might be able to transition into a more productive path. First, they had to acquire the resources to become men capable of providing for their families by going to college or working. While this kind of masculinity—working hard, finishing school, and providing for families—could place the boys on a better trajectory, the boys encountered various obstacles on this path. Riverland lacked entry-level jobs and community programs to help this group of youths transition back into school, and the schools' zero-tolerance policies led many to be expelled for gang activity. Frequently, the boys viewed school as a place that targeted them as criminals and cared little for them. Thirty-two of the fifty-seven had dropped out of school or had been kicked out, and twelve told us they dropped out because they felt they did not belong or school officials did not care about them. On the streets, police gang units stopped, "tagged" (entered into a gang database), harassed, and arrested the boys, sometimes for something as simple as walking to the store to buy groceries.

When the boys attempted to get jobs or complete school, their avenues for opportunities often turned out to be dead ends. The realization that they were not able to be the kind of man mainstream society expected them to be inflicted stress, anger, and pain. As a result, they forged alternative forms of manhood—forms that often stressed being tough, gaining status and respect, and, like the police did onto them, demonstrating dominance over others.

Synthesized Masculinity

Men gain masculine esteem and status from the acknowledgment of other men (Cooper 2009); but with limited access to traditional avenues used to accomplish this task, the boys negotiated alternative masculinities, particularly through interactions with police officers. The boys adeptly demonstrated aspects of dominant, street, working-class, and subordinate masculinities in a complicated enactment. In response to police mistreatment, they practiced deviant behavior (ignoring police officers, attempting to block police from taking pictures, protesting their potential arrests, and so on), symbolically defying domination, control, and harassment without a fight and, thus, gaining masculine status and esteem.

Officers used toughness, dominance, disrespect, humiliation, and aggressive force to try to control boys upon arrest—a tactic that often proved counterproductive. With every negative interaction and perceived wrongful conviction, youth lost respect for the cops and the legal system. Those who encountered negative police interactions felt they received wrongful treatment in the courts, and, conversely, those who experienced positive or neutral interactions, perceived the justice system as treating them fairly, despite similar "juvi" or jail sentences.

Although the boys aspired to achieve dominant forms of masculinity, they embraced synthesized forms. For example, fifteen-year-old Elias defined being a man:

> A real man is a leader not a follower. He has backbone. He stands up for himself. He is able to protect himself. He doesn't go out and look for trouble just because. He lives for his own satisfaction and no one else's. He works when he can, and when he can't find work he finds a way to make it work.

For Elias and other South Riverland boys, this redefined masculinity was achievable. They could be leaders, they could stand up for themselves, and they could be themselves—guys who appreciated a street orientation. With this synthesized masculinity, they could fill the gaps to access resources and mitigate race and class privileges they seemed to lack. The performances of synthesized masculinities differed by boy, unique to each of their situations and perceived strengths and weaknesses.

Men who constantly face challenges to their masculinity or find that "masculine resources" are in short supply may turn to criminal behavior (Messerschmidt 1999):

> Masculinity challenges arise from interactional threats and insults from peers, teachers, parents, and from situationally defined masculine expectations that are not achievable. . . . Masculinity challenges may motivate social action towards masculine resources (e.g., bullying, fighting) that correct the subordinating social situation, and various forms of crime can be the result. (13)

Indeed, criminal activity constitutes a gendered practice that men rely on to communicate their manhood. As such, crime is more likely to occur when men need to prove themselves accountable to strict gender expectations, based on how they interact with social institutions such as law enforcement (West and Fenstermaker 1995). Therefore, an examination of the boys' interactions in their community can reveal how the criminal justice system shaped their development of masculinity.

The young men I followed constantly faced challenges to their manhood on the streets through such interrogations as "Is he really a homie?" or "Is he really a man?" Those who could not measure up were stigmatized or victimized. At the core of growing up in their community, the boys felt a constant necessity to prove their manhood. Institutions also often challenged their masculinity in the attempt to reform them. They may have been told they were not "man enough" to have committed a crime or that once "in the system" they risked being emasculated. In response to gendered institutional practices, they boys synthesized new practices, identities, and models of masculinity.

The underacknowledged collateral consequences of the criminalization and punitive social control of inner-city boys include constant surveillance and stigma imposed by schools, community centers, and families; permanent criminal credentials that exclude them from the labor market; and the boys' mistrust and resentment toward police and the criminal justice system (Rios 2011). As I followed the South Riverland boys, I found an additional consequence: the development of a specific set of gendered practices, heavily influenced by their interactions with police, detention facilities, and probation officers.

For example, negative encounters with white female teachers often called up a scenario of an "angry male of color" attacking a "white damsel in distress." Encounters with police often became a contest to see who was the "bigger man," and probation officers interacted with the boys in either a motherly or a heavy-handed way. These patterns of punishment provided a constant backdrop against which these young men exhibited their understanding of masculinity.

Race determines the treatment a young person may receive in the criminal justice system, but masculinity plays a role in whether the person desists or relapses into recidivism as they pass through that system. For young black and Latino men, pervasive contact with the criminal justice system produces hypermasculinity, or an "exaggerated exhibition of physical strength and personal aggression," often in response to a gender threat, "expressed through physical and sexual domination of others" (Harris 2000). I found that the criminal justice system encouraged hypermasculinity by threatening and misunderstanding these young men's manhood. Detrimental forms of masculinity reflecting violence, crime, and counterculture were reinforced through youths' negative interactions with police, juvenile hall, and probation officers. Although we think of law enforcement as *policing* such behaviors, I discovered that police often played a crucial role in *producing* them and their attendant meaning and significance.

Masculinity, Criminalization, and Punitive Social Control

Gender expectations shape human behavior, and each person is subject to a system of accountability based on gender, race, and class (West and Fenstermaker 1995). The boys in this study were inculcated with hypermasculine expectations that often encouraged behavior in conflict with dominant institutions. But with probation officers and police, the boys had two choices: engage in a battle of masculinity or submit to authority. The choice was a lose-lose predicament, and they knew it. If they acted tough, officers might hesitate to harass them, but they just might get arrested. If passive, they risked humiliation. Caught between these positions, many acted out their frustration through drug use or violence. The "default" manhood they knew best involved masculine resources they could purchase on the streets.

Peers, family, and neighborhood institutions impose multiple litmus tests that men must pass to win "real man" status, according to many contemporary urban ethnographers. For example, Elijah Anderson (1999) described "young male syndrome" as the perceived, expected, and often, necessary pressure to exhibit a tough, violent, and deviant manhood in order to receive and maintain respect. Although other men can prove their masculinity through their ability to make money and buy consumer products, poor young men must rely on the tools they have—toughness, violence, and survival (Pyke 1996). Even young women in poor neighborhoods learn to rely on this form of hypermasculinity for their own protection and to gain respect (Jones 2010; Rios 2011). They face a double bind as they seek to meet feminine gender expectations and simultaneously adopt tough masculine behaviors necessary to survive on the streets (Jones 2010).

Most violent youths are not psychopaths, but rather, "overconformists to a particular normative construction of masculinity" (Kimmel and Mahler 2003, 1440) defined by toughness, dominance, and the willingness to resort to violence to resolve interpersonal conflicts. Many of the South Riverland males were acquainted with the mainstream culture's expectations for boys like them—work hard, obey the law, and accept their subservient social position. Indeed, some had fathers or father figures who emulated these values, and some boys sought to embrace this masculinity in an effort to reform. But where could they find viable jobs to "prove" they were hard workers? In a deindustrialized society, proving masculinity through success in jobs involving physicality and muscular prowess is less possible for larger numbers of men (Kimmel 1993).

Gang-associated boys very quickly come to realize that positive, working-class masculinity does not provide the resources to survive on the streets, a place to which they constantly return. In their attempts to manage young men's criminality, institutional authorities (police officers, teachers, probation officers, judges) resort to practices heavily influenced by masculinity. In response, these young men are socialized to specific meanings of manhood at odds with those dominant institutions that seek to control them. Without viable employment or guidance, they are led right back to the seductive arms of hypermasculinity.

As an example of how this process works, criminologists have found that police academies train officers to practice a rogue and hostile masculinity (Prokos and Padavich 2002), which reverberates in the inner city. Angela Harris explains, "Police officers in poor minority neighborhoods may come to see themselves as law enforcers in a community of savages, as outposts of the law in a jungle" (quoted in Prokos and Padavich 2002, 442). In this context, punitive police treatment of men of color is, not only racial violence, but also gender violence.

Young people in South Riverland encountered these forms of violence regularly from police and consistently reported interactions with disciplinary authorities at school and with police from an early age. They learned that "being a man" meant not relying on law enforcement, learning to take a beating from police, and—sometimes—to desist from committing crime and to resist the seductions of street life. But as they practiced their masculinity on the streets, the boys' interactions with authorities also informed and reinforced their identities. Targeted as likely criminals, they encountered an expectation that limited their mobility, affected their families and relationships, and increased their chances of ending up in the criminal justice system. The masculine behavior and ideals the police and others promoted were often less available for these boys than authorities seemed to imagine. As a result, hypermasculinity served both as resistance and self-affirmation. In turn, this survival strategy created a self-fulfilling prophecy, a ready-made rationalization entitling the system to further criminalize and punish them.

The boys in this study, however, did not passively submit to police officers' challenges to their masculinity in all of their interactions. Rather, they demonstrated active resistance through developing "synthesized masculinities"—a process that made masculinity more attainable. Neither dominant nor subordinate masculinity alone could explain the meanings that gang-involved Latino boys navigated and the actions they created. The boys constantly negotiated subordinate, street, working-class, and dominant forms of masculinity. With few resources and facing diverse demands from families, police, and schools, they often perceived failure as inevitable. Therefore, demonstrations of masculinity were a last-ditch effort to acquire social status and alleviate subordination. Even more than race or class, masculinity was for these boys a coping mechanism in a world that seemed to wage attacks on them at every turn. Masculinity was a vehicle to alleviate social marginalization and subordination. Unfortunately, women and others were often the victims of these young men's synthesized masculinity, as the men used violence to battle against emasculating control.

This study and others underline the need to change the punitive and gender dynamics of policing and the toxic definitions of what it means to be a man (Bradley and Danchik 1971; Cooper 2009). Extensive law-enforcement training programs should be designed to challenge a macho police culture and address racial, gender, and class stereotypes. Officers also could benefit from training on how to communicate effectively even when their authority is challenged and to avoid acting on the premature presumption of violence.

Listening to the stories and viewpoints of these gang-associated young men, we can easily think that police officers operate under malicious intent. But do they? Are they simply out to make young people's lives miserable? How do police officers view young people they interact with, and would understanding these interactional dynamics provide tools for schools, law enforcement, and policy makers to engage more positively and productively with youths? I rode along with police officers in South Riverland to try to answer these questions and to understand the police officers' viewpoint. The following chapter examines these interactions from a patrol-car perspective.

CHAPTER FIVE

The *Mano Suave* and *Mano Dura* of Stop and Frisk

(with Samuel Gregory Prieto)

While in their patrol car, two officers noticed a young Latino male spinning himself around in circles with one arm looped around a telephone pole. This behavior appeared out of place to Office Langham of the Gang Suppression Team (GST). He quickly made a U-turn and steered the patrol car to the curb. In a split second, the boy bolted down the alleyway into the South Riverland neighborhood, and Langham's partner, Officer Grant, hopped out to chase him. Langham radioed for backup and a canine unit and accelerated up the block. A minute later, police cars screeched into the neighborhood from all directions. Some officers drove slowly block to block; others searched alleys and backyards on foot looking for the boy, tightening the police net on the perimeter. Suddenly, Langham's radio crackled, and an officer panted that he had spotted the boy and was in pursuit.

Langham drove toward the location where the officer detained the boy in a backyard at the end of a cul-de-sac a few blocks away from the place where the chase had begun. Other patrol cars flooded the cul-de-sac, and fifteen officers leaped out and ran to the backyard. Before long, the officers escorted the boy in handcuffs toward the patrol cars. Sweating, his face smudged with dirt, he appeared to be in his late teens or early twenties and was wearing a striped polo shirt and baggy black jeans.

Officer Grant explains that the young man was high on meth; he was really "coked out." He states that the young man tried to swallow the drugs he was carrying, but began to choke. He eventually coughed it up. His eyes are really big and his pupils are dilated; he blinks often and deliberately. They seat him on the curb and a middle-aged white officer starts to make small talk with him.

Officer: "Where are you from?"

Boy: "From here."

Officer: "Are you okay?"

The boy nods.

Officer: "Did you watch the Super Bowl the other day?"

The young man replies in a an anxious but logical manner. Discussing the rival teams and some of the plays that were made. The officer replies with details about the game and the young man responds. The conversation appears more like game talk between two friends rather than small talk between a person under the influence of drugs and the officer that arrested him.

Compared with the frenzied, hot pursuit of this youth, the officer's tone and modality was calm, cordial, and conversational, as the officer quickly shifted his interactional stance based on the circumstances.

During our thirty-two ride-alongs with police officers following four years of observations among the youths, we observed forty-six police encounters with Latino, gang-associated youths. We were able to discern two distinct, contrasting approaches the officers employed that we call *mano suave* (soft-handed) and *mano dura* (hard-handed) policing. Just as the youths could enact "drift" or model shifting, in their day-to-day lives depending on their environments and the associated interactions, police officers also might move between punitive and supportive roles with youths. They vacillated between these roles according to a logic that was at once protective and suspicious of the youths. Even when officers hewed to a *mano suave* approach, they often misinterpreted the youths' interactions and intentions and, in the end, switched to a more punitive stance to compensate for their uncertainty. Thus, even when they attempted to be more lenient, they were bound to the punitive cultural context of law enforcement. This process of cultural misrecognition and misinterpretation created misframings in the police-youths interactions that could potentially escalate to the pernicious fire of brute force, entrapment, and even death.

Most police stops of Latino youth in this study did not end in arrest or gun fire, but officers referred to the case of the boy spinning around the telephone pole and the ensuing chase as a justification for stopping similar-appearing young men. For example, boys who looked *cholo* were often targeted—and victimized—as if *cholo* style were a clear indicator of drug use or drug dealing. And while officers appeared consistently to attempt to engage with these young men in positive ways, their efforts were undermined by their deep-seated suspicions or fears that the youths were high or guilty of some larger crime.

Officers assumed a boy they stopped would turn and run or be insubordinate. But even a youth's silence or irresponsiveness could quickly provoke a change in the officers, from a soft-handed approach (positive greetings, docile body language, polite mannerisms and language such as please and thank you) to hard-handed action (cursing, raised voices, and physical threats and contact). Understanding this transition from *mano suave* to *mano dura* and the conditions surrounding these interactions sheds light on how police officers—even the cordial ones—might participate in brute force or even deadly fire.

Punitive Drift

Juvenile delinquents navigate between extremes in their behavior—law-abiding and criminal—and commit crimes after preparation and desperation (Matza 1964). In this "drift," preparation occurs when the person realizes a criminal act is achievable and feasible, and desperation arises from an extraordinary event or fatalism, which activates the will to commit the crime (Matza 1964). Matza found that youths who feel they have been treated unjustly experience diminished commitment to law-abiding behavior, but then feel guilty after committing a crime, which, in turn, compels them to curb their criminal acts.

We found that police officers also appeared to drift between conventional and nonconventional behaviors, between problem-solving approaches and punitive treatment of the neighborhood youths. But we found the quality of their interactions, not just guilt, could determine the direction and frequency of their vacillation. And for the officers, drift was not between law-abiding and criminal behaviors, but rather between respectful and punitive treatment of young people. When and why do police drift toward punitive treatment, such as verbal abuse or physical force? When do they drift back? What factors influence violent or forceful interactions with police? What are the determinants of lenience or severity in police interactions with Latino youth?

We found that officers' drift between *mano suave* and *mano dura* was informed by their cultural misrecognition of young people's actions. Just as the interactions between teachers and students at Punta Vista became entangled in the interplay of misunderstood intentions, so too did the police officers' interactions with youths on the streets tend to break down through cultural misframing. For example, during a ride-along, an officer spied a youth drawing on the wall of the bathroom facility in the park and instantly assumed the boy was preparing to tag the wall with spray paint. The officer stepped on the gas pedal, hit the curb, jumped out of the car, and dragged the kid to the ground. After the chaos, the officer realized the boy was participating in a legitimate art project. He was staging the exterior wall so that a local artist could paint a mural he had been contracted to create through a community center program. The fact that the boy was dressed in baggy clothes penciling a design on the wall created an impression for the officer that the boy was a tagger who needed apprehending quickly before he could run off.

Informal Surveillance

To understand why police officers drift between *mano suave* and *mano dura* approaches, we must understand both the conditions under which these interactions occur and their content. Officers rely on formal and informal surveillance of the Latino youths they suspect of wrongdoing. These "check-ins" take three distinct forms: the passing "check-in," the parole or probation check, and the "Terry stop" (referring to the *Terry v. Ohio* Supreme Court case where the court ruled that it is not unconstitutional to stop and search a suspect on the street without probable cause to arrest). Officers considered the passing check-in to be a somewhat benign way to touch base and eliminate any potential flares that could escalate into something problematic, dangerous, or criminal. They viewed the parole or probation check as a preventive measure to control crime by keeping close tabs on youth who had prior records of delinquency. The Terry stop was a deliberate action to address something perceived as an immediate or imminent threat. A Terry stop is a short detention of a person by police on reasonable suspicion of involvement in criminal activity. These stops are commonly referred to as "stop and frisk." Pretext stops are typically stops executed for minor traffic violations in order to investigate more serious criminal activity. For the purposes of this study, we are using the concept of pretext stops as a practice that extends beyond the traffic stop—they can also be non-traffic stops including stops while walking, shopping, or being at school. Pretext stops, beyond the definition of the law, are stops conducted for suspected minor offenses in order to uncover criminal activity. Hereafter, we use Terry stops, pretext policing, and "stop and frisk" interchangeably.

We witnessed dozens of such stops during our ride-alongs, and in none of these cases did the GST officers actually witness illegal and organized gang-related activity. When officers had no legal reason to stop someone, they frequently relied on pretext to "check in" with the young Latino males on whom they wished to keep tabs. Some of these boys were on parole, but the assumption seemed to be that they all were and the GST officers had a duty to monitor their behavior daily. Operating on a logic of prevention and paternalism, police officers performed this "regime of checks" based on the asymmetrical power relationship they maintained with the youths.

Regarding the content of the interactions, the youths' compliance or resistance seemed to influence but not determine the officers' drift toward *mano suave* or *mano dura* behaviors. When a youth complied with an officer's demands—especially if the youth had some previous relationship with the officer—his cooperation might soften the officer's tone, or more substantially, moderate the severity of the consequences the officer meted out. During a search or arrest, officers were more lenient if they perceived a youth to be basically a "good guy." Therefore, the officers' relationships with youths and their perceptions that a boy was either fundamentally good or reprehensibly irretrievable could influence their drift between *mano suave* and *mano dura*. For example, the following incident involved Jason, one of the young men in the study, who was loitering on a street corner:

As we turned the corner, Officer Myers goes from speaking in a drowned out, tired voice and yawning to an alarmed, excited voice. "That's your boy!" He tells his partner, Officer Acevedo. "We better check up on him. This kid is bad news." As he speaks louder, the car screeches to a stop. Officer Myers opens his door ready to step out of the car and approach Jason. Jason looks alarmed and ambivalent. It looks like he wants to run, but recognizes that will land him into more trouble. He appears nervous and anxious, he starts pacing, making no eye contact with officers.

Officer Acevedo turns to Myers and says, "Hold on, man, I just checked on him yesterday. He's good, man, he's good." Immediately, Officer Myers's demeanor changes. He turns his cold stone face into a smile and throws up the peace sign to Jason. Officer Acevedo rolls down the window and asks Jason, "You OK, man?"

Jason sighs, "Yeah, I'm OK. You guys scared me man. I thought you were trying to arrest me."

"For what? You got something?" asks Officer Acevedo.

"You know I'm clean, sir, you know I'm clean, sir!"

Both officers chuckle and so does Jason. The car drives away. Jason walks away in the opposite direction.

Sometimes, the underlying suspicions officers had about youths were confirmed; other times, not. But especially when they were not, we observed Latino youths felt "hassled," which put additional strain on an already tense dynamic. If youths protested or expressed even a hint of outrage at being hassled, police typically drifted to a *mano dura* stance. The officers' cultural misrecognition contributed to the conditions that spurred the youths' negative reactions, which, in turn, pushed the officers toward *mano dura*.

In some instances, police reacted to visibly unlawful—albeit fairly benign—behaviors that signaled alcohol or drug use. But for the most part, informal surveillance and check-ins constituted the bulk of the interactions police had with Latino youths in South Riverland. As such, we focus on the conditions and content of those interactions in which clearly illicit, gang-related activity was not observed. Yet some interactions between the police and the youth evolved and escalated as if there was significant criminal behavior on display. To be sure, the chase that occurred with the youth allegedly high on methamphetamine was an unusually dramatic example of a police response to illicit activity. Here was one youth behaving erratically and responding to police officers in a highly reactive manner that served as a case study for understanding the punitive extreme of the *mano suave–mano dura* continuum.

Regime of Checks

The bulk of officers' time and energy was spent conducting formal and informal surveillance of the Latino youths whom they targeted in their gang "suppression" work. These "passing check-ins" seemed to be relatively positive encounters when Latino officers patrolled together or alone, rather than when they patrolled with white offi-

cers or when white officers patrolled together or alone. Latino officers seemed to fall into the trap of miscommunication less often,
perhaps because they understood the boys' unspoken cues. They
could discern when *cholo* style was just aesthetics and when it promoted crime.

Interactions during passing check-ins were typically fleeting,
cordial encounters between the police officers and a youth who often
was someone the officers knew relatively well. The officers techni-
cally did not detain the youth, but made their presence known.
On one ride-along, for example, Officers Acevedo and Hernandez
noticed a youth named Javier sitting on a bench. They stopped the
car, and Officer Acevedo rolled down the car window, called the boy
by name, and asked what he was doing there. After a few moments,
the officer said, "Stay out of trouble," and the patrol car pulled away.
Innocuous as this check-in with Javier may have seemed, it fore-
shadowed the quality of future interactions between him and law
enforcement, as well similar encounters with other youths.

Officers usually initiated the interaction casually, as if saying
"hello." Depending on their perceptions of the circumstances and
the youth's response to their overtures, however, these interactions
could resemble an interrogation. For example, Officer Acevedo
pressed Javier to clarify how he walked from his home neighborhood that was a twenty-minute drive from South Riverland. But
even when the interactions were cordial, fleeting, and mundane,
the officers were, as Officer Myers put it, "hungry for information,"
and the interactions were intended to serve the officers' primary
purpose: surveillance and data collection. This case illuminates
one of the contradictions of procedural justice practices also known
as community policing or legitimacy policing. The goal is to build
trust and prevent negative interactions with police. However, we observed that cordial and polite policing can also contribute to punitive treatment and harsh outcomes. When used for data collection
and surveillance, cordial policing makes community members more
suspicious and mistrusting of police. The assumption is that police
are being friendly in order to find incriminating information or to

cultivate an informant that might be labeled a snitch in the community, one of the worst labels one can garner. In addition, no amount of cordial treatment at first contact by police will guarantee that the interaction will not turn sour, or brutal, or lethal. And police politeness will not eliminate harsh laws or extreme sentences for minor offenses—perpetuating the national phenomenon of mass incarceration.

Police officers used formal surveillance technology to support their informal monitoring. When they recognized a passerby on the street, they frequently pulled out of the flow of traffic and entered the person's name into the police database accessed through a laptop mounted to the dashboard to check for any outstanding warrants.

One evening, at approximately six p.m., Officers Langham and Grant pass a man on the street [whom they know, and they enter his name into the computer]. A warrant comes back, [two to three months old], connected to a felony conviction . . . because the man had not checked in with a parole officer.

The officers pull into an alley where this man is walking. . . . [He] may have just come from the nearby corner store since he is carrying a plastic bag. The man wears his hair in a long black braid that extends down to his lower back . . . [and] is wearing dark jeans and a white fitted ("wife beater") tank. We approach him in the patrol car from the rear.

[The officers stop] their vehicle perpendicular to the alley entrance, creating a barrier to traffic. They call out to him by name, get out of the vehicle, and search him, pinning his thumbs behind his back in their usual way. They do not find anything illicit in their search, and the man is compliant when the officers call out to him to stop. . . . [As they are arresting him for his] outstanding felony warrant, . . . two other units arrive on the scene . . . another police patrol and . . . a White Crown Victoria, [carrying two men who] . . . wear dark cargo pants and blue polo shirts that say probation in yellow letters. They carry badges on their belts.

Over the years, the GST and other police officers built experiential knowledge augmented by the formal criminal database network they could access from the field and to which they could contribute. For instance, when officers learned young men's nicknames in the course of a stop or arrest, they added this information to the list of monikers in the database. When they discovered a fresh tagging, they photographed the graffiti with a camera that used GPS technology to pinpoint its location in the database. With this information, they could track patterns and concentrations of various gang-related tagging. Officers also regularly communicated with probation officers and sheriff's deputies to coordinate searches and arrests. Quick access to this police database was key in Riverland, a relatively small town. Because officers often recognized youths by name, they could determine prior to initiating contact whether individuals could be stopped because they were on parole, probation, or had an outstanding arrest warrant.

Officer check-ins typically led to a search if the officers knew or learned that the person was on probation or parole. In addition, individuals on probation or parole were subject to coordinated and unannounced checks of their homes and warrantless searches as part of the terms of their release.

During a ride-along, we noticed a young white man in his late twenties riding a bike. His head was shaved, and he was wearing baggy jeans and a faded T-shirt. The patrol car pulled up behind him, and officers asked him to get off his bike, sit on the curb, and show them his identification. The man told them he was on parole.

An officer asks for what? The man responds, for arson. The officers both laugh out loud. One says that typically people do not just volunteer that information. The man shrugs, but does not respond.

Officer Grant, holding the man's ID says, "you know the usual routine," at which point the man turns around and places his hands behind his back to be searched. The motion is so nonchalant it appears rehearsed. They search him by pinning his thumbs together behind his back while Officer Grant runs his other hand over the man's body. They search the bike too, looking under the seat, poking the padded part of the handlebars to see if anything is hidden there. As they are making small talk and waiting for his information to come back from dispatch, he explains that he has one more year on parole for this arson case.

They ask what the case of arson was about: Why did he burn down whatever he burned down? The man responds that he would rather not say, and the officers laugh a bit more.

An officers asks whether he was "white power" [a white supremacist prison gang] while he was serving his time. The man responds with a tentative yes, stumbling over his words a bit. He adds quickly that he did so out of necessity: in order to form an association with other inmates so that he could protect himself. Dispatch finally radios back. The man has no violations or outstanding warrants, and so they let him go and the man bikes away.

As in this example, probation and parole status facilitated the officers' surveillance, widening their ability to conduct searches, although this particular incident yielded nothing illicit.

Pretext as Practice

Academics have struggled to define and measure pretext policing and racial profiling (Gabidon and Greene 2008; Rios 2011; Wordes and Dynum 1995). For this study, we defined pretext policing as instances in which officers observed minor illicit activity that would not normally require any intervention and used the incident as justification for questioning individuals about some crime or potential crime. Rather than an exception to standard police practices, we found that pretext policing was standard operating procedure for the GST officers during our ride-alongs.

On a late afternoon, the officers receive a "service call: gang types refusing to leave." Someone has reported tagging at a local school.

The graffiti appears gang-related, and so two other officers who have already responded to the scene call the GST officers. When we arrive, a middle-aged, white officer and middle-aged, Asian American officer brief GST Officers Acevedo and Hernandez. . . . As they talk, they stand between the two patrol cars parked parallel to one other. No one is sure who is responsible for the tagging, and the description that the officers have of the perpetrator or perpetrators is vague: Latino youth wearing dark, baggy clothes. A small group of teenage Latino men are hanging out in the parking lot of a community center adjacent to the school. They sport the same style as many of the young Latino men their age: baggy jeans, baggy shirts, close cut hair, and visible tattoos. The middle-aged white officer tells the two GST officers that they should go talk to the youth in the parking lot.

The middle-aged white officer and the middle-aged Asian American officer are joking about how to approach these youth. The white officer jokes about another officer whose notion of "consensual contact" is to say, "Sit down!" he imitates sternly. As he says this he steps toward the hood of his car with his hands behind his back and bends over slightly, mimicking a search. Evidently the officer they are joking about is quite harsh with these young men. Officer Acevedo, who I noticed had not been laughing as heartily, responds, "I don't do that." The white officer retorts, "I know you don't, but you should!"

They go on to reiterate that no one actually saw the guys who tagged the wall. But the Asian American officer observes that the young men hanging out in the parking lot are "smoking underage" as he holds an invisible cigarette to his lips. He does not elaborate further, but he seems to be very clearly suggesting that underage smoking could be a pretext to inquire about the tagging that just occurred. The white officer goes on to say that it is their job to hassle these guys.

Although Latino officers participated in the same drift between *mano suave* and *mano dura* policing as other officers, they often hesitated or questioned the practice more than white officers. However, their relatively critical stance did not prevent them from policing the boys in the very same way as white officers. All officers are embedded in institutional structures that compel and coerce them to "do their jobs," which may include punitive strategies that conflict with their personal morals but align with their professional roles and social norms in policing. The older white officer tells the Latino officer that he is not harsh enough with the gang kids. Possibly socializing him to crack down harder on the boys because that's what he "should" be doing.

Officers' perceptions of their work and their role in it shape their policing style. In this instance, the older white officer saw his primary function as "hassling" these youth, hewing more closely to the *mano dura* approach, while the GST officer rejected that approach. Notably, the middle-aged Asian American officer who arrived first on the scene supplied the GST officers with the pretext for questioning the young men: underage smoking.

Two GST officers and their sergeant, Sergeant Steele, are on patrol. They notice a white SUV that is traveling quickly down a winding road in the foothills above the city. As it passes us, one of the officers notices that there are four young Latino men in the truck. They speed up so they can follow it . . . and as Officer Langham drives, he says he definitely sees "four heads" in the car. Officer Grant is running the plates from the passenger seat as we are following the SUV. Their sergeant is riding along tonight as part of his routine supervision of the GST unit. We sit next to each other in the back of the patrol vehicle. We follow them for approximately five to ten minutes. Near the end of this time, Officer Grant reports that the plates came back "clear and valid," indicating the registration is up-to-date and there are no warrants associated with the vehicle or its owner. Abruptly, or so it seems to the officers, the SUV makes a quick turn into the driveway of a house situated in the hills above the city. The officers pass them, turn around, and drive back past the house where the SUV has parked. One of the officers says he thought he recognized one of the young men in the car and that person may have been on probation. Sgt. Steele replies, "He's already off the road."

The sergeant's comment suggested that since the SUV was no longer on the road, there was no longer any legal reason to justify a stop. This deliberation and consideration of possible pretexts typified "officer talk" during patrols. Day-to-day activity involved finding creative ways to make officers' targets more accessible.

As we patrol the mostly Latino [section] of the city, both officers say aloud that they think they recognize a Latino male riding his bike down the street. Just as they recognize him, the man turns a corner and proceeds in a different direction. Anticipating his path, Officer Grant circles the block, pulls up behind the man, and then makes a quick right to continue following the man on the bike.

Officer Grant notices the man riding his bike on the sidewalk [a city violation] and notes this aloud. He turns to Officer Langham and says, "There you go."

In this case, Officer Grant noticed a technical violation, which provided justification for the stop. As with many other interactions, actually witnessing gang-related criminal activity was not necessary; instead, officers' perceptions or previous knowledge that the youth was involved in gang activity could trigger a stop. (We will return to this example later in this chapter.)

The officers confirmed they used pretext to justify their stops, although they never described their actions in those terms. Rather, they saw technical or other violations as an important enforcement tool in their surveillance and data collection, the bulk of their gang-suppression work. Even when officers had the right to stop someone on the street because the person was on probation or parole, they often used another reason that would allow them a longer time to detain that person and ask questions. Thus, a technical violation of the law became the occasion for executing the "real" work of the police.

Police interactions with these youths give us a portrait of race relations in the United States. A wealth of scholarship has explored and highlighted the disproportionate effects of the prison-industrial complex and the war on drugs on youths of color, resulting in disproportional sentencing and police brutality. In Riverland, officers' targeting youths for surveillance and interactions, we could see how the "reasonable suspicion standard" (Seth and Novak 2014) could gradually lead to legal legitimation for using race in policing (Epp et al. 2014). Racial profiling has become part of the coming-of-age experience for young U.S.-born men of color (Rios 2011; Goffman 2014) and a "racial naturalization" for immigrant men (Carbado 2002). Race, especially signified through skin tone, certain clothing, hair, and tattoos, signals to police officers that these young men deserve scrutiny, even—and perhaps especially—when they are doing nothing illegal.

One evening, in the police break room, Sgt. Timmons discussed his philosophy on policing:

Sgt. Timmons is open, expressive, and confident: a people person. While his posture and tone suggest the stoicism and severity characteristic of many officers' professional personas, he is not nearly as guarded as many of the other officers we have encountered. Without solicitation, he reflects on his time with the police department. He discusses the department's relationship with the Latino community. This leads him to reflect on how they decide which young men to target.

He says, "If you are wearing baggy pants and sporting tattoos and I have the choice between looking at you and an old lady, I am going to look at you. That is just the nature of the job." Sometimes, he says, . . . the officers are wrong.

Sgt. Timmons normalized the role of race in policing. As officers targeted people and not behavior, the "nature of the job" inevitably dictated that they focus on young Latino men who "look the part": brown skin, baggy clothing, a shaved head, and tattoos. Faced with the choice between someone obviously not engaged in illegal activity and someone the officer "reasonably suspected" was making trouble, race became a significant factor in the officers' formulation of their suspicion.

> In a separate incident, Officers H and E reflect on a check-in from earlier in the day with a young man on a small footbridge . . . [whom they say] . . . is "assuming the role more and more." This is the first time that they have seen him with his head shaved and he increasingly refuses to talk to them, even when they are just "checking in."

To neglect to respond to officers' questions is read as a sign of criminality for young men of color. The irony is that many community advocates, activists, and attorneys counsel marginalized young people to know their rights and to refuse to talk to police with the intent not to incriminate themselves. However, in practice and interaction, the refusal to answer questions leads to dire consequences for marginalized young people, including further scrutiny, harassment, citations, arrests, brutality, and even death at the hands of police. The irony of being poor and racialized is that demanding their constitutional rights can cost them their liberty or life.

Officers often noted whether a young man's head was shaved or his hair had grown out since they last surveyed him, markers that suggested gang affiliation or an effort to disaffiliate. The officers used racialized cues like these to confirm or allay their suspicions, and, therefore, when young men grew their hair out to cover tattoos on the scalps, officers regarded them more positively. Race and style were central to the officers' daily work, despite formal and public pronouncements to the contrary.

Justifications of Power

Riverland police officers used three rationalizations to buttress the "regime of checks" that we witnessed time and again during our ridealongs: prevention, paternalism, and power relationships between police and youths (presumptively symmetrical). Officers first cited prevention to justify their approach, a quality that is largely immeasurable, and then underpinned this prophylactic reason with paternalistic regard for gang-involved youth. Finally, they believed police objectives aligned with those of community advocates, indicating a latent assumption that power between police and youths was basically commensurate. In other words, youths and authority figures engaged in a somewhat "give-and-take" relationship in which both groups did what they could to prevent future arrest.

In one instance, as we were walking through a park on the south side of town, a "hot spot" for gang activity, the officers offered a rationale for preventive measures as an approach to stemming criminal behavior among gang-associated youth.

> Officer Grant says that he understands that these young men feel like the police are "fucking with them." But often these checks, he says, are to take weapons off these guys. Indeed sometimes they find knives, which Officer Grant says prevents future crime. For that reason, they feel like these stops are worth it. . . . He says that this kind of policing is hard to quantify, even though only a fraction of the stops may result in arrest. This is what he calls "proactive policing." When they take knives off these guys, there is no way to quantify or measure what kind of harm that prevents in the future. He says that for many of these guys, being in a gang and having an interaction with a police officer is like a business. They get pushed into crime because of the community they were born into, but you get used to these interactions. They become part of the routine, part of your daily life. And so, in some ways it is just business as usual when these searches occur.

One former gang member paraphrased what an officer told him: "The gang is a full-time job with no benefits." He took this idea to heart and repeated it to other boys he thought were delving too deeply into gang crime. In this sense, some of the lessons the officers imparted during their *mano suave* approach with the youths made a difference. The same was not true for the *mano dura* approach. Instead, the youths developed resentment and often resisted even if it meant being arrested. The problem was that young people could never predict whether an officer would turn on them, drifting from cordial treatment to punitive treatment.

Nevertheless, police officers believed their check-in stops were beneficial because of the occasional drugs or weapons they were able to confiscate. Taking these things from the young men before they could use, deal, or harm someone else demonstrated a good outcome—an unknown, but potentially significant deterrent. With this logic, there was no way to know how many violent acts would have been perpetrated with a knife or a gun had an officer not checked in.

In addition to prevention, the officers viewed their surveillance in the neighborhood as benevolent paternalism. They perceived their relationships to these young people almost as an overseeing parent, an attitude that served as an ideological foundation for this regime of checks. For example, one evening the officers were patrolling an apartment building that appeared to have once been a motel with two floors of units arranged around a central parking lot. As they pulled the patrol car into the lot, they noticed a young man sitting on a stool outside a ground-floor apartment, drinking a beer. The officers called the man by name and approached him.

As soon as this young man sees them, he ducks inside the apartment, leaves his beer on the chair, and closes the door. The officers approach, knock on the door, and call him by name. But there is no response. Officer Grant threatens him, "Open the door or we'll open it."

They continue to knock on the doors and windows, calling the young man by name in an angry tone of voice, but he never responds or opens the door. The officers linger outside for five to ten minutes before [they] give up and leave.

As we are walking away, the officers are talking about how frustrated they are with this young man. They do not understand why he would not just talk to them. Officer Langham says that sometimes he feels like these guys are "like his kids" and he feels frustrated by them. He wants them to behave in a certain way, but they resist. He says that next time they see this young man on the streets, he expects he will tell him something like, "I didn't know you were there," lowering his voice to imitate the voice of someone who sounds stupid. He is anticipating and deriding a lie that they expect this young man will give them. Officer Grant says this kid is not supposed to be drinking as part of the terms of his probation. Officer Langham responds, "I just get so disappointed." They say that sometimes they feel like one of these young men is beginning to turn things around, but when they respond to the officers in the way this young man just did, they feel let down.

When the youth did not comply with demands, the officers' personal and emotional responses perpetuated a more paternalistic, *mano dura* approach. They wanted the youth to stay out of trouble, and his noncompliance both provoked their personal frustration and suspicion that he was up to no good, reinforcing the pull toward paternalistic intervention. But their frustration with this youth's resistance, despite the officers' "just wanting to talk," ignored the circumstances under which an interaction with a police officer transpires, as well as the myriad reasons why youths might view such conversations as much more than "just talk."

The notion that officer check-ins were merely invitations to "just talk" was one of the most frequent euphemisms we encountered in our fieldwork. Failing to recognize the dynamics of power at work in their interactions with youths, officers presupposed a degree of parity that simply did not exist, and, therefore, they were surprised when the youths were not compliant. For example, over dinner at a fast-food restaurant, Officer Grant recounted a time when he asked a "tatted up" man to talk for a moment:

In the course of their exchange, Officer Grant came to find out that this man is the head of an organization working locally with gang-involved youth to pull them out of the life. Upon learning this, Officer Grant reports engaging him in a discussion about the way the police approach these young men. The man he has just stopped says the kind of hassling that he has just been subjected to is detrimental to these young men. From Officer Grant's perspective, he is just talking or checking in. He asks the man how he contacts these young guys. The man responds that he will walk up to these young men on any street corner and simply begin talking to them and try to get them involved in his organization's programs. Officer Grant says this is exactly what the GST does; they approach these young men on the street and ask to talk to them just like this community advocate does in order to keep them from engaging in criminal activity. He sees them as equivalents, but notes that he and the man disagreed on this.

Many times officers told us their goals were similar to ours (as researchers and youth advocates): to gather information in order to understand how best to help these "kids." Clearly, most officers thought of themselves as service workers who were trying to help; however, under pressure from the public to eradicate gangs, they resorted to punitive tactics that turned good intentions to bad practices. Although the police believed they shared the same goals as community advocates, they did not occupy the same institutional position. In fact, as armed agents of the state authorized to use violence, the police stood far apart from community advocates—their institutional power separated by a chasm that belied the innocence of the overture to "just talk." And so, police-youth interactions were steeped in cultural misrecognition as officers drifted fluidly and sporadically from *mano suave* to *mano dura*, from help to hinder.

Cultural Misframing and Drift: From *Mano Suave* to *Mano Dura*

A key determinant of an officer's drift between *mano suave* and *mano dura* was the officer's misrecognition and misframing of a youth's interactional and cultural cues. A young person's apparent effort to "get straight," as officers called it, especially compliance with law enforcement's demands, influenced an officer to drift to the *mano suave* approach. But *mano suave*—leniency and respect toward youths— was never decoupled from the immediate threat of force, nor did the approach bar the officers from fulfilling their law-enforcement obligations. In our ride-alongs, we observed that *mano suave* did not prevent officers from executing a warrant or making an arrest, yet the approach could preclude force or yield forms of leniency that mitigated the long-term legal effects of the encounter. In this sense, *mano suave*, what some call legitimacy policing or community policing, can be a wolf in sheep's clothing; sometimes the wolf stays hidden, but other times the wolf uncovers itself, leading young people deeper into the criminal justice system, with a velvet hand—a cordial policing approach—leading the way.

We observed the *mano suave* approach one night as GST officers monitored a faded Oldsmobile parked at a gas station. Several minutes into the surveillance, the officers believed the four Latino men in the car had noticed them. Three of them walked off into the night. As the car drove off, the GST officers followed, and eventually pulled the car in a residential neighborhood.

The officers have the driver step out of the car. They search him and find, among other things, a spoon wrapped in a white cloth. They seat him on the curb. The man is approximately five foot six, 170 pounds. His head is shaved, he sports a moustache, and he has a sheen on his skin; it looks as though he is sweating lightly. On the back of his neck he has a tattoo that says, "I had a choice, but I chose wrong."

Officer Grant is making small talk with the man, asking him about his kids and his siblings, . . . [and] tells him, "You don't want them to follow your path." The officers have placed the contents of the man's pockets on the trunk of his vehicle, including the spoon. A K-9 [canine] unit arrives . . . [to search the vehicle]. I hear the man ask to be let go. Officer Grant responds, "I'm holding you responsible for your actions." Later Officer Grant reports that he knew that the man was high on heroin. The man asks for a drink of water. [Officer

Grant retrieves a cup and] . . . holds it out to him so the cuffed man sitting on the curb can drink. Officer Grant is talking to the man again, saying if you smoke or drink and drive, "What do you want me to do?" There are rules. If the man respects Officer Grant, Officer Grant will return that respect. He will treat him right, but that does not mean he can let the man go.

Despite the national trend in procedural justice, legitimacy policing, and community policing, no amount of cordial and polite policing treatment will mitigate the dire consequences of punitive laws and harsh sentences that have led the United States into mass incarceration. One example is the criminalization of drug addiction and the long sentences that drug addicts receive after being caught with miniscule quantities of drugs. This public health issue has been treated as a crime issue and as such has led to the incarceration of individuals with conditions that could be treated by therapists and social workers. Sociologist Waverly Duck (2015) has brilliantly demonstrated how this criminalization of drug addiction impacts entire neighborhoods, weakens positive social networks, diminishes social institutions and government support, and leads communities to have to fend for themselves. Legitimacy policing, done right, is only the first step in addressing the massive problems of mass incarceration, racial disparity in incarceration, and disproportionate police brutality and harassment in communities of color in the United States. Policy changes must also follow. Such recommendations are discussed in the conclusion.

Returning to the young men arrested for driving under the influence, the officers placed the man in the patrol car for the ride to the county jail. During the trip, Grant sat in the back, making small talk with the man. They talked about a recent gang-involved fight in the neighborhood and about the man's family. GST officers regularly chatted like that with young men they detained, asking about their families, recent arrests, and other youth in the community. Grant said the purpose was to calm the man down and de-escalate the situation, and because "I care." Officers log the information they glean for the future, to try to push the young man into making better decisions. For instance, if officers know that a young man has children, they might mention that fact the next time he is detained, leveraging the information to urge the person to stay out of trouble: to do right by his kids.

Grant went on to describe a previous encounter with the same man. While in prison, the man was set to get a tattoo that would have covered parts of his face and hands, but the process was interrupted, and the final design was far smaller than planned. Later, the man told Grant he was glad he didn't get the larger tattoo down his face, a comment that Grant said was evidence that the man was beginning to come around and understand what it would take to live "straight." Grant said, "This is the way you chip away at them over time."

> Officer Grant says . . . he hopes to encourage this guy to leave the gang life, to grow his hair out so you don't see the tattoos on his skull. He says to stop "looking like a fucking gang member" so that he is able to get a good job and provide for his family. When he says, "look like a fucking gang member," it's that he recognizes the way other people view this man and he wants him to change his appearance somewhat so that he can have opportunities that he doesn't have now.

In this case, the officers went easy on the man, asking him only to sign a form admitting he had violated his probation, instead of charging him with a new crime, which likely would have sent him back to prison. *Mano suave* was visible in the officers' interactions with the man and the legal penalties they chose to issue. They talked respectfully to him, offered him a drink of water, and insulated the man from a more protracted interaction with the legal system. They used discretion in the consequences they meted out, undoubtedly because their perception was that the man was trying to "get straight." In addition, he apparently had responded honestly to their questions. His compliance, coupled with their positive view of him, influenced the officers' drift to *mano suave*.

Conversely, we witnessed the officers' drift to *mano dura* when youths talked back to the police or resisted or refused their demands. In many cases, misrecognition was a key contextual element at work in these situations. When officers misrecognized or misread the youths' cultural cues and used those cues to target them for suspicion, the youths became angry and defensive. As a result, the youths perceived they were being treated unfairly, which strained their relationships with the police, undermined the trust the officers sought to cultivate, and diminished their effectiveness.

We described a previous incident in which Grant and Langham were on patrol when they recognized a man on a bicycle and began to follow, looking for a pretext to stop him for a check-in. In this case, the man objected strongly to the officer's profiling him and clearly viewed the stop as harassment. The young man was almost six feet tall and weighed about two hundred pounds. Tattoos covered parts of his arms, calves, and neck.

Officer Grant opens by saying, "I want to let you know why we're stopping you. It is because you were riding your bike on the sidewalk." He continues in the way he normally does, saying that he just wants to talk for a minute. "What is your name?" The man does not give his name and immediately becomes aggravated.

The man challenged the officers' reasoning, pointing out that other people were riding bikes on the sidewalk and they were not stopped. He accused the police officers of deliberately targeting him.

"And you were following me. I saw you several blocks back, and then when I saw you right here, I saw that you turned right really quick." He says that he was just going to the store. . . . "You're labeling me," he tells Officer Grant. "You're labeling me."

The man's direct challenge and the charge of racial profiling spurred the officers toward *mano dura*.

As the man became more combative, Officer Grant retorts in a stern and impatient tone of voice, "Okay, we're going to search you." He pins his hands behind his back, pinning his thumbs together with one hand as he searches with the other. He turns up a pocketknife that he flicks open and shuts maybe ten times. He tells the man that the knife is illegal because it can be flicked open in a single movement. The man retorts that it is not illegal. Officer Grant affirms that it is, in fact, illegal.

During the interaction, the man recognized the officers and pointed out to them that they had pulled him over several weeks earlier as he was driving with his family after taking his son for a haircut. This very recent stop was obviously still quite clear in the man's memory and seemed to account for his negative reaction and his charge of being targeted. He continued to reiterate that he was just going to the store for his kids, that he was a hard worker with a full-time job and had not been involved in anything illegal for many years. At that point, Officer Langham stepped in with a *mano suave* approach.

Officer Langham . . . seizes on the fact that this man has a family and says, "I've got kids, too. How many do you have?"

The man replies, "Three."

Officer Langham says, "I have four and I can respect any man who is doing what he has to in order to make ends meet for their family."

The man reiterates, "I work. I work and that's it."

He says he doesn't hang on the corners. Officer Langham responds by saying he respects a family man. As the man is talking to Officer Langham about his family, he calms down. Officer Grant interjects that he needs this type of interaction from him at the beginning the next time. Officer Grant says they're just trying to check in and keep things safe. All he wants to do is talk to the man and get to know him. The man says he did his time and now his number one concern is his family. They both say that they can understand and respect that. They return his knife and do not issue a ticket.

Officer Langham's intervention de-escalated the situation as he attempted to relate through their shared struggle to provide for their families. From law enforcement's standpoint, nothing came of the stop: The officers learned nothing about any significant criminal activity. However, in the man's eyes, the incident reinforced the capriciousness of racial profiling.

The misrecognition and misframing inherent in pretext stops and the taint of racial profiling define the parameters of interactions like this one. Although individual responses to police overtures influence officers to drift between *mano suave* and *mano dura*, the officers' own misrecognition and misinterpretation critically structure the interactions from the beginning. In this context, officers do not regard gang-associated youths' unsurprising rejection of racial profiling as a legitimate form of dissent, but view their resistance as an occasion for even more invasive encounters—encounters that often mark young people with labels that stick across settings and into adulthood.

Mano suave and *mano dura* policing—that is, the policing that ambiguously drifts between cordial and polite policing to punitive policing—is not a sustainable, moral, or efficient model. Those officers that are able to practice a more stable form of *mano suave* policing, also referred to as community or legitimacy policing, are able to garner more respect and credibility with community members. But being nice alone will not offset the deluge of punitive policies, such as arrests for minor infractions and harsh sentencing for small-time drug offenses. Policies must change in order to provide officers more flexibility in using their discretion to help community members reintegrate into society after they have broken the law. In addition, the incentive system that rewards officers for hypermasculine, rogue mistreatment of suspected criminals must change. Instead, police departments must implement reward systems that promote those officers that demonstrate a genuine commitment to improving interactions with community members and finding creative ways to bypass a culture and system of governance dominated by *mano dura*.

CHAPTER SIX

Immigrant Targets

By the time he was seven years old, Jorge was well acquainted with death and abandonment. Born into poverty in Mexico City, he and his older brother were left behind with grandparents when their parents migrated to the United States. But life's tragic uncertainties soon forced Jorge to rely on his own wits.

> My dad came [to the United States] first because he murdered someone in Mexico and he had to get away. . . . My mom came here after, had my little brother here, and then went back. Then my dad went back. Then I lived with my grandparents. My grandpa got shot when I was a little five-year-old kid. My grandpa and me were so close, so attached. Then his nephew shot him in the head. So he died, and then that was a really sad moment in my life. Then my grandma got in a car accident and she rolled down the hill, and so to save her son, she threw him out the window. So she got out, but the truck was coming from the air and picked her up and just destroyed her. So both my grandparents fucking died, and those are the people who took care of me. Then my mom left us in Mexico and my dad so we didn't have anyone there. We lived with my uncles and we were little kids—that's kinda like crazy that you're a little kid—and I was fucking seven years old living by myself in Mexico just kind of fending for my own. My mom would send us money, but it's not like you have someone there to really watch you.

When Jorge was nine, his mother sent for him and his older brother. Their uncle accompanied them to Tijuana, a twenty-hour bus ride from Mexico City. There, a *coyote* (human smuggler) picked them up, locked them in the big trunk of an old car, and drove off without giving them any details.

> I thought we were going to die. It was hot and bumpy. It took for-ever . . . like two hours. We got out in the desert and some other guy started running. He said, "*Pegen se bien, cabrones, o se van a perder y se van a morir*" [Stay close, fuckers, or you will get lost and die].

Jorge recalls running for what seemed to be hours with no water until they came upon a dirt road where another old car, trunk open, awaited. Hours later, they were delivered to their mother in Los Angeles. Once in the United States, Jorge moved into the South Riverland neighborhood, where he, like many other Latino youths, began to encounter layer upon layer of illegality. Each layer imposed its own stigma and sanction that limited Jorge's ability to break free and prove himself worthy.

By the time he was ten years old, Jorge was hanging out with the gang-associated boys who were his neighbors and part of his child-hood playgroup. Pressured to conform to the ubiquitous south side gang culture, Jorge also felt excluded in many ways. Other neigh-borhood youths looked down on him because he could not speak English and was undocumented. He said, "If anything, you have to put in extra work [acts of bravery] to prove yourself when you are *mojado* [derogatory for undocumented]. You have to be crazier and then that's when they give you respect." He was not initiated into the gang until age fifteen:

> JORGE: Yeah, the only reason I didn't get jumped in [is] because I had gotten stabbed and the day they were going to jump me in they were jumping people in and that's when they jumped in my brother. Some guy . . . he told everyone else, "you guys better not take a swing at this fool 'cause he's fucked up." I had gotten stabbed in my arm and my stomach.
>
> V.R.: How did it happen? Tell me the story.

JORGE: They [rival gang members] see me walking. I had long socks [wearing baggy shorts with long socks to the knee, a gang-associated style in Southern California]. I was all gangstered out. They started whistling and hit me up. . . . I was going to run because there was a bunch of them, but . . . I didn't want to run and have them fuck my brother up. I started talking shit to them and they crossed the street and my brother crossed the street. And they were like let's get down one-on-one, and there was like five of them, and they were like OK one-on-one. And as we were walking they started stabbing me and started fucking us up and then I don't know. . . . I didn't noticed I got stabbed until I looked down at [my] shirt—I was wearing a white shirt—it was all red. It didn't feel like I got stabbed, it just felt hot, really, really, really hot. And as time went on I was walking around bleeding 'cause they hit an artery. I was bleeding crazy and my fucking vision started going more black and more black. I passed out and just woke up to all these cops around me asking me what happened. They try to say I was gonna get charged for a gang fight even though I didn't even get a chance to throw a punch.

After the stabbing, Jorge was interviewed multiple times by police; a day after his release from the hospital, he was stopped by police officers three different times. They wanted to know when he had been "jumped" into the gang (an act of initiation), and demanded to know his gang moniker. Frustrated, Jorge said his gang name was "*Koke*," the nickname his family had given him as a child in Mexico, even though he was not yet a gang member. With no evidence beyond a style of dress, a stabbing, and a childhood nickname, Jorge became "*Koke*" in the gang database. In the eyes of law enforcement, he was a gang member even before his peers had initiated him in.

After his recovery, Jorge returned to school only to discover that his stabbing and the gang initiation (by the police and then his peers) had set him up for another layer of illegality. Here, I use the term "illegality" to refer to the process in which people, and not just their behaviors, are labeled illegal by institutions, the law, and civil society. I build on the work of Menjivar and Kanstroom (2013) who understand illegality as a process created by the law that enters the conventional cultural world. I conceive of illegality as a culture and logic that penetrates various institutions in society, embedding itself in the everyday practices, interactions, and discourses of individuals engaged in such institutions. At school, because of Jorge's extended unexcused absences, the administrators told him that he had broken the law by being truant and that he could not possibly receive credit for the semester and encouraged him to attend the alternative probation school, Punta Vista, which had a more flexible credit system.

But at Punta Vista School, Jorge found opportunities to connect with older boys from the gang. Soon he had forged a deeper bond with them and began to put in work with them on behalf of the gang. Instead of working with Jorge to achieve success, the school essentially knocked him down by labeling him excessively truant and removing him from earning a public education, which, in turn, made it more difficult for Jorge to obtain the resources he needed to build a beneficial life.

When youths like Jorge are expelled from school, they find that opportunities to acquire the required credit hours to graduate are more limited. If they go to continuation or alternative school, they enter a different realm with its own rules imposed by school and other gang-associated peers. Breaking a rule at the continuation school leads a youth one step closer to the criminal justice system; breaking a peer-imposed rule means being an outcast or a victim. Once police set their sights on a troubled teen, the youth draws more scrutiny, surveillance, and police stops. Probation status allows law enforcement to check on, stop, and search a young person at any time of day. These are the layers of illegality that make young people feel at a loss, hopeless, and unacceptable, and this effect is even more drastic for those who are undocumented, adding an additional layer of illegality.

From the beginning, Jorge persistently challenged the Punta

Vista School principal, clowning around with her, calling her names, and making jokes about her. Infuriated one day after Jorge told her she looked like a "tweeker" (drug addict) because she was extremely thin, the principal threatened to call his probation officer. Then she upped the ante and invoked his undocumented status. Threatening like usual to call her brother, a sheriff's deputy, to arrest him, she said, "You know, once they take you in, you will be deported!"

Jorge shifted his gaze to his feet, as shame swiftly turned to anger. Glancing to the right, he noticed two girls standing next to him, and looking left, he caught my gaze. His eyes turned back to the principal, his face set with pain. Before his emotions could boil over, he laughed it off, and replied, "Then I'll get to take *unas vacaciones* [a vacation]!"

Jorge's undocumented status placed him in a paradoxical predicament at school, with law enforcement, and among peers. He had to navigate under the radar to avoid deportation, but he had to push the edges of criminality to prove himself to his peers and on the street and to show he was a worthy individual among those of Mexican descent who are born in the United States. Young people on the streets internalize the formal and informal labels that family, community members, and the state give them—illegal, illegitimate, deviant, criminal. As such, they police each other's illicit status. Being rendered "illegal" by the state leads to being treated as illegal by society. The de jure label by the state facilitates the cultural conditions for the de facto use of "illegal" as a mechanism for creating symbolic understandings of people in the community as more of a threat and less deserving. On the streets, young people police each other's illegalities.

Jorge described his peers' expectations for him this way:

> They expect me to do anything else that nobody else will be doing like being out there fighting, doing crazy stuff. . . . People get treated differently on the street. It depends on who's your family and who you're related to—yeah, yeah! You have to try harder to prove your-

self on the streets if you're *mojado* [derogatory for undocumented]. You have to, you know, do some crazy shit to prove yourself.

One day, when I entered Punta Vista School to conduct observations, I was greeted by Jorge's booming voice as he yelled with excitement: "I'm going back to school! I'm going back!" After four months at the continuation school, he had demonstrated a desire to change and had been granted permission to return to Riviera High School. To the youths, leaving Punta Vista meant feeling they were "back to normal," "back to school," back to a world that viewed them as deserving positive treatment. "You've changed your attitude and you are doing a lot better than before," the principal told him as he walked down the hall and back into class. Beyond having to prove his worthiness on the streets among his peers who also thought of themselves as outcasts from school, Jorge had to prove his innocence and worthiness to return to his regular school.

I interviewed Jorge two weeks after he had returned to Riviera High. His enthusiasm had already subsided. Jorge described waiting for a white classmate after school with the intention of beating him up because of a comment he had made. However, before the fight could occur, the school had notified Jorge's probation officer, who interviewed the white student to see if Jorge had threatened or attacked him.

I shadowed Jorge as he navigated various classrooms, trying to understand what had changed his optimism about high school to feelings of exclusion and degradation. The high school's student population was 40 percent white and 48 percent Latino; however, most students in Jorge's classes were Latinos. I counted only three white students out of more than 130 of Jorge's classmates. The exception was his history class, where he was one of two Latinos. His classes seemed particularly chaotic—students talking throughout instruction time, walking in and out of class unannounced, and using cell phones at will. Teachers seemed ambivalent and disengaged.

Jorge's relationship with his history teacher, Mr. Sweeney, was particularly antagonistic. Whenever Jorge walked into class, Mr. Sweeney greeted him with a frown. He often stated loudly, "Are you gonna give me more trouble today?" and patted Jorge on the back, a condescending gesture Jorge attempted to avoid.

One day, as I greeted some boys in the school yard between classes, a song blared from a fancy black-and-silver Magnavox boom box placed on a chair near the door of Mr. Sweeney's classroom: "She's a maniac, maniac, and she's dancing like she's never danced before . . ." Mr. Sweeney was notorious at the school for playing loud music between classes, primarily selecting songs of the 1980s from the likes of Michael Sembello and other one-hit wonders. Students found the music annoying (as intended), but also comedic. A white student who felt guilty enough to approach me and tell me about Mr. Sweeney's "racist music" explained, "He calls his music 'bug-a-thug' music. He gives us extra credit for bringing CDs with the most annoying music possible." He proceeded to pull out a CD he had created especially for Mr. Sweeney, labeled with a Sharpie, "Bug-a-Thug greatest hits."

Later, Jorge and other Latino students also told me that Mr. Sweeney's bug-a-thug music was designed to dissuade gang-associated Latino boys from hanging out near his classroom, which was located at a key nexus point where three buildings connected. During lunch and between classes, mass concentrations of students accumulated in this small zone. The forty or so gang-associated Latino boys at the school gathered adjacent to Mr. Sweeney's class to catch up and people watch, and he hated it. His tactic failed to work as intended. The boys ignored the music, but they got the message: They were unwelcome and detached from the collective effervescence that Mr. Sweeney created among white students who provided bug-a-thug CDs. At least fourteen times, I witnessed white students walk up and hand Mr. Sweeney a CD, sparking laughter among them.

Mr. Sweeney's classroom walls were covered in historical posters from various time periods, early twentieth-century food advertisements, quotes from "Founding Fathers," and World War II news

headings and images, including a picture of a zombie-looking figure
sticking his middle finger in front of his face with a Nazi swastika
prominently tattooed on his forehead. Just above Jorge's seat in the
far right was a poster that resembled the yellow caution sign commonly seen along interstate highways near the U.S.-Mexican border.
The sign portrays silhouettes of a man, a woman, and a child running. The man is shorter than the woman and is leading the pack;
his hair is poufy, his nose pronounced, and his torso is thicker than
his waist and appears a bit paunchy. The woman wears a dress and
has an elongated jaw line. She holds the child by the wrist, pulling
her along, as the girl's pigtails fly out behind her. The sign was created by the California Department of Transportation in the 1990s to
warn drivers about possible border crossers, undocumented pedes-
trians frantically running across the freeway to make their way into
the United States.

But Mr. Sweeney's poster was different. Behind the frantically
running trio hovered the figure of the grim reaper, arms extended,
reaching out toward the family. Jorge described his interpretation
of the sign:

It's lame. That's like us. *Ese buey quire que nos lleve la chingada* [that
idiot wants us driven to hell]. He doesn't believe that we belong here
so he wants us chased out. . . . I don't feel good in his class, and even
outside of his class I have to hear his stupid music.

Negative images and interactions with school personnel conveyed the clear message to youths that the school was an anti-*cholo*,
anti-immigrant, anti-Latino space. Sometimes, the interactions
were so disrespectful that youths could scarcely contain their rage.

One morning, I noticed Julio in the hallway near the school's
main office just after the late bell had rung. The morning sunlight
backlighting the school's poorly lit hallways made it difficult to identify faces, but Julio was easy to spot. His six-foot-four, 240-pound
figure cast a distinct shadow.

"Julio, is that you?" I whispered.

"Yeah, is me! Whaaat uuup Dr. Rios?"

He was wearing a Lakers insignia baseball cap and a sleeveless Lakers jersey with "Fisher" on the back. A tattoo of a fire-encircled dragon was wrapped around the length of his thick, flabby arm. As I began to ask Julio if I could shadow him after school, Mr. Wiedman, a physical education teacher, suddenly interrupted. "Where the hell have you been!" Mr. Wiedman scolded. The teacher was as tall as Julio, but much thinner. Looking shaken, Julio shrugged his shoulders. Wiedman erupted again:

Just 'cause you're big and bad you think you can act like you run the whole freakin' school? I know other teachers will put up with you, but I won't. If you want to be a thug, school ain't the place for it.

With fists balled and head bowed, Julio walked away. When I caught up to him, he murmured, "Dog, that was nutty. I wanted to punch him in the face, but I don't want to get kicked out again. I don't want to go back to camp" (a locked-down juvenile detention facility set up as a military boot camp aimed at reforming nonserious offenders).

Although most teachers at this high school were not so confrontational, they did employ multiple methods that tended to imply rejection of disreputable young people. These practices included stern body language, ignoring the boys' presence in class by not talking to them or making eye contact, and discretely requesting that school security pull them out of class. I witnessed teachers telling students that because of truancy or missed assignments, they had already failed the course, conveying the message that their further attendance was a waste of time. For three of the boys, that statement was a clear signal to skip the class and instead loiter outside or down the street until the next period—behavior that placed them at risk for victimization or police harassment, citations, and arrest.

The negative interactions, rejection from authorities, and layering of illegality led to the youths detaching from school and drifting toward alternative, more accepting cultural frames elsewhere—

primarily in the streets. There, they could act physically tough, pretend to be regular consumers of alcohol and marijuana, and exaggerate their role in gang crime and violence. They carried this narrative—more posturing than reality—back into the classroom. Indeed, I observed that many of the boys who were kicked out of school were not heavy drinkers or smokers, nor regularly involved in fights, hard-core gang crime, or violence. Instead, they were caught between two worlds.

The boys commonly expressed two aspirations: to graduate from high school and at least attend community college, and to prove themselves relevant to others so they could maintain a credible reputation in their neighborhood. These aspirations often collided: Why attend school when you could hang out with your homies all day long? Still, many boys persisted in regular school attendance despite the seductions of the streets. Unfortunately, school officials seemed to be fixed on the boys' "street" identities, or other imposed layers of illegality, ignoring a more telling message: Despite the strong pull of the streets, these boys continued to show up to class.

By letting implicit and explicit biases structure their perspectives about these "at-risk" students' abilities, intentions, and aspirations, educators placed additional barriers in their paths and set a series of negative outcomes in motion. Labeled unruly and truant at school, youths hung out on the streets, where police felt justified in stopping and frisking them at will, inevitably leading to harassment, citations, arrest, or even brutality.

Once a youth was arrested, the legal system scrutinized his legal status, and the court could impose incarceration or probation. Undocumented youths could be reported to Homeland Security and deported. Probation meant the loss of many basic civil rights, such as the requirement for police to have a warrant to search their home or the home of anyone they were visiting. In addition, probation officers and police were permitted to stop and frisk them at will, exposing the youth to greater risk of additional incarceration.

As these young men encountered more layers of illegality, they were even more vulnerable to crime and victimization. With the odds stacked against them, they could easily feel hopeless about their futures: Even if they finished school, they still faced difficulties getting a job because of documentation or arrest records; even if they successfully completed their probation program, they still faced peer pressure on the street to prove themselves. As Jorge described, undocumented boys had an even greater challenge to prove their manhood, loyalty, and respect on the street. In Riverland and in cities across the country, entire groups of young people are considered, not only illegal by the justice system, but also socially illegal by their peers and community. Many turn to crime and violence in search of a sense of belonging. Vincent, a seventeen-year-old push-out who claimed gang association explained:

> I just want people to respect me. The homies, they gave me a hard time but after a while me *respetaron* [they respected me]. I knew how to prove myself to them. . . . I am still learning how to prove myself to the system, though.

Illegality and Liminality

Youths who experience multiple layers of illegality as outcasts from family, the school, the police, and conventional peers are vulnerable to becoming involved in delinquency and crime. The gang provides an entryway to a community of belonging, but street status and "perks" are awarded for a price: proving one's worthiness to older, more established street-life oriented individuals.

Alvaro grew from a short, chubby "wannabe" to a full-fledged "shot caller." From an early age, he admired gang-associated youths from South Riverland. "Like my aunt's boyfriends and my older sister when she used to kick it with . . . like she used to know guys from the south side. They would wear clothes like that. I was like, damn, I want to be like that." Before he was even a gang member, school officials labeled him one. After his first expulsion at age fourteen, he enrolled at Punta Vista and spent several years navigating the alternative education system and the streets bearing the labels of an outcast and delinquent. The pull of street culture combined with the push of punitive school culture opened up an avenue of street opportunity for Alvaro.

Now fifteen, Alvaro was learning the hard lessons of the street. Short and chubby, older youths made fun of him, telling him he looked like a baby. I met Alvaro in front of the community center where I was observing a group of boys. James, a charismatic seventeen-year-old introduced us. "This is my 'son,'" he said, patting the younger boy on the head. Then James shoved Alvaro and kicked him in the ass.

"Dog, you're so dumb, they flunked you out of ninth grade," another boy taunted.

Alvaro had recently been expelled again for punching a boy from a rival neighborhood, which the school considered a gang assault and a violation of zero tolerance policies. Now on the streets, Alvaro suffered abuse from his peers even as he tried to find a place for himself. Taking their cue from the verbal abuse, the group of boys surrounded Alvaro and started smacking him and kicking him around. Looking at me, one boy laughed, "He's like our soccer ball. Wait up, homie, let me go score a goal!" The boy ran up to Alvaro and kicked him so hard I heard a thud from where I stood ten feet away.

Alvaro tried to laugh off the abuse, but as he walked by me, I could see the tears in his eyes. Some older boys tried to console him, telling him the rough treatment was just part of life. One day, he will be the older one, one of them explained, but for now he has to put up with them fucking around. James wrapped an arm around Alvaro and said, "Kick back! We are just showing you love. All you have to do is show all these lames that you can handle the heat. That's when they respect you."

Almost three years later, Alvaro was back in school, one of the oldest of the boys from the neighborhood still enrolled. He had clearly learned the gang's lessons well. During my observations at Riverland High School, I noticed a new pattern: He was no longer anyone's punching bag, he had a troop of younger boys who looked up to him. Wherever he walked, they followed.

At lunchtime, he simply nodded his head and one of the tenth-grade boys, Joey, heeded the wordless command. Joey obediently got up and returned with the boy Alvaro had indicated.

"Why did you let that lame disrespect you?" Alvaro asked the boy.

"Who?" the boy said, puzzled.

"The one over at the game."

I learned later that Alvaro was referring to a boy from a rival high school who had called this boy a name. The boy had ignored the insult, but not Alvaro. For Alvaro, no one from his neighborhood—gang-associated or not—should put up with disrespect.

The boy seemed panicked at Alvaro's rebuke. Stressing the point, Alvaro pointed a middle finger in the boy's face and ordered, "I better not hear that you let those lames disrespect you again." The boy nodded his head several times, and Alvaro sweetened his instruction with an invitation: "What are you doing after school? Come chill with us."

Alvaro had succeeded in recruiting his own cadre of younger boys. He ordered them around, verbally insulted them, and even kicked them in the same way I had witnessed him being kicked a few years earlier.

For countless pushed-out urban youths like Alvaro, the gang serves the double function of pulling in those who have been targeted as outcasts and socializing them through an internal disciplinary mechanism that teaches them submissiveness and how to prove their manhood and worthiness in the gang. However, the gang is not an autonomous institution with an isolated social order, but an integrated, interdependent institution impacted by the cultural forms, social order, and rules operating in schools, law enforcement, and other relevant institutions. Thus, those boys whom conventional society treated as outcasts were often outcasts within the gang hierarchy, until they could prove themselves.

Institutional labels matter in the real world. Once an individual has been given an official label by the law, like "illegal" or "felon," these labels follow him or her across institutional settings and social interactional terrains, creating systems of interpretations, symbols, interactions, and practices independent from the law but very much contributing to punitive, demoralizing, detrimental outcomes. This explains the common processes uncovered in this study where schools resemble prisons, peers resemble police, and teachers resemble immigration officers. Dominant systems, in this case punitive laws and policies, become embedded and embodied in individuals (see Bourdieu 1977). These individuals might be representatives of the system—that is, authority figures—but they might also be everyday people—parents, peers, neighbors—that are influenced by the system and in turn adopt the prevailing views, perspectives, ideologies, or frames generated by powerful institutions and officials.

These punitive de jure and de facto outcomes breed resistance in targeted individuals. For the youths in this study, the more legally, socially, and institutionally marginalized they became, the more the street-life frame became a perceivably viable alternative. Not only was this a matter of rejecting their rejecters, it was also a matter of reconstituting themselves as dignified, multidimensional individuals that defied the overbearing stereotypes, labels, and treatment they experienced.

In Jorge's case, his official criminalized status as an "illegal immigrant" under federal law rendered him a target for disproportionate ridicule and bullying among the boys in the neighborhood and in the gang. Alvaro was a target among his peers because of his physical and educational deviance: he was young, short, chubby, and "kicked-out." Both boys had to overcompensate to prove themselves because they did not fit the gang's conventional definition of a member. These nonconventional boys typically ended up committing the hardest crimes and gaining the most notorious reputations on the streets.

The difference between the gang and other institutions is that the gang provides deviants with an achievable way to manage the stigma it initially imposes. Labeled a gang member by the police, a youth is unlikely to shake the stigma for years, but those labeled "weak" by others may be granted a clear path by the gang for proving their worth through "putting in work." The gang's "probation" may lead to future higher status and respect, in contrast to the legal system's probation that often sticks for years at a time and perpetuates a spiral of criminality. The more that the system pushes one out, the more likely that one will experience social outcasting by relevant others.

Labels like "at-risk," "gang member," "illegal," "truant," and "criminal" provide the symbolic resources for other institutions, including the gang, to create hierarchies, and, in turn, determine which youths are relegated to committing the hardest crimes or receiving the worst victimization. Although neighborhoods play a key role in the trajectories of inner-city youths, institutional context also matters. The quality of the interactions youths have with institutional authorities and the labels they are given mediate the frames these youths adopt. In turn, frames influence the behavioral outcomes young people perceive for themselves. Institutions that provide unambiguous rules, a chance to prove worthiness, and accomplishable goals are the institutions that win the hearts of the masses. In Riverland, the gang was the most maneuverable institution that these youths encountered.

Adolescent development is affected by the labels and treatment imposed by various institutions. The quality of interactions between youths and institutional authority figures impact a young person's well-being, future aspirations, perceptions, and attitudes. Interactions and labels can determine whether youngsters end up attached or detached from school, family, and law enforcement. Negative labels such as "illegal," "at-risk," "dropout," and "gangbanger" accompanied by negative treatment—a process I refer to as layers of illegality—have the power to diminish young people's motivation and self-efficacy and cause them to drift into various deviant frames available to them, including a gang identity where they find a sense of belonging and worthiness. Institutions play a powerful role in delegitimizing, and in determining the kinds of cultural frames available to, and adopted by, targeted populations.

From Culture of Control to Culture of Care: Policy and Program Implications

Two years into my study, Jorge, one of the most delinquent, drug using, defiant boys in the sample, decided he wanted to leave the gang life behind. One day, out of the blue, he decided to confront his homies about his decision to leave the gang. He waited for a Friday evening when a large number were gathered. He told me the story, a few days after this event. "I just got tired of it, Rios. *Esos bueyes ni me acen el paro* [those fools don't even back me up]. Then one day I thought, man, I could get deported. This shit is nutty. . . . I just went up to them the other day *y les dije* [and I told them], 'gangs are for immature people.'" Jorge explained that his homies, a large group of over twenty, acted perplexed and shrugged their shoulders but no one confronted him. "They just told me, you gotta do what you gotta do homie!" He left thinking that things were all good, that his friends would respect his decision. Many of them did. But some were upset about his way of going about leaving the gang. Jorge believed that his notoriety and reputation of being one of the toughest guys in the neighborhood and the first one to attack rival gang members would shield him from repercussions. However, a few weeks after dropping out, one of his homeboys who was driving an automobile spotted Jorge while he rode his bicycle. He tried to run him over. Jorge jumped off; the car trampled his bicycle.

Jorge experienced many attacks over the course of a few weeks. Around this time, I would pick him up and take him to lunch or on drives around town to check in with him and make sure he was OK. During a car ride with him, Jorge recounted to me a major life decision he had recently made. One day, the guys came to his house and threw rocks on his window. They broke the kitchen window where his mother was standing. Jorge was infuriated. He contacted one of his childhood friends, a white kid from a middle-class family. Jorge's friend, Miles, had access to a collection of guns owned by his father. Jorge asked Miles if he could borrow the "AK," an assault rifle. Miles agreed. Jorge told me, a few days after this event, that Miles had given him the rifle. Jorge wanted to use it to teach the guys a lesson. He would wait until they gathered at the park and shoot them up.

As Jorge waited for the right time to confront his old homies, he got a call from his mentor, Jacob, an ex-professional hockey player that had retired in an affluent part of Riverland. Jorge met him through the local community center, which tried to match local professionals with at-promise youths (here I am referring to young people labeled "at-risk"; "at-promise" is a more appropriate term). The mentoring relationship was very informal. They had lunch once a month or so, whenever Jorge felt like responding to Jacob. Jorge explained to me that he decided to go to lunch with Jacob this time because he was stressed about possibly shooting his old friends. He asked Jacob to give him advice on his situation, without telling him he had possession of a gun. Jacob told him that he had made an important life choice and that he was a step closer to becoming a man of honor. Someone that could stand alone, that did not need a gang to back him up. He told him to hang in there and that he believed in his ability to transform even further. Jorge was touched by the conversation, by Jacob's ability to connect with him, to see his potential. "*Le llame al pinche guero y le di su pinche cuerno* [I called the damn white guy (Miles) and gave him his damn AK]." Jacob's conversation had somehow inspired Jorge to do the right thing. Jacob served the role of delivering a positive interaction to Jorge and affirming his multiple selves in a critical juncture in his life. While Jacob did not have a clue that Jorge was ready to shoot up the neighborhood, he was committed to being consistent with Jorge and showing him that he believed in him, that he represented an adult that cared for his well-being. Imagine how many shootings could be prevented if more young people had a mentoring lifeline like Jacob. Unfortunately, there are very few programs in poor communities aimed at providing quality mentoring for gang-associated youths. Even in Jorge's case, his mentor was a self-driven volunteer who took the initiative to approach the community center for mentoring opportunities. The program was very informal. What if more young people like Jorge encountered more formal mentoring programs, employment opportunity programs, and other social and educational programs?

Jorge is now a floor manager at a fancy restaurant in the heart of Riverland. He makes a decent salary there and has avoided the deeper pitfalls of the street life. He wears a crisp white shirt, a black tie, fitted dress slacks, and long hair parted and combed to the side, with a shine to it.

≈ ≈ ≈ ≈

Interactions matter. The quality of interactions between the youths in this study and authority figures played a major role in their chances of overcoming adversity and proving negative labels wrong. Young people who encountered or perceived they had encountered more negative interactions with authority figures ended up experiencing higher incarceration and dropout rates. Those who encountered positive interactions after having experienced negative ones were able to find more hope for attaining an education and employment and for desistance from crime.

Resources also matter. Interactions are one kind of resource. How authority figures label and engage with young people often determines the kind of emotional energy created for their decision-making and thought processes. Negative interactions become negative resources because they often influence the punitive treatment process. Positive interactions can provide a better outlook for young people and an authority figure's openness to grant access to material resources, like a job or an educational credential.

So what can we do as policy makers, educators, police officers, or practitioners to capture that sense of hope and possibility for these youths and redirect our efforts to guide their development and life trajectories toward more positive outcomes? How can we recognize the process of creating human targets and cultural misframing in the various institutions that impact the well-being of young people? And see these as factors that derail youths' genuine attempts to desist from crime and excel in school or at work? In the same vein, how can we acknowledge authority figures' gestures to relate to youths when so many of these interactions are fraught with contradictions and hidden biases? How do adults get it so wrong in their interactions with youth—and how can we get it right?

It seems almost cliché to say that adults misunderstand teenagers since adolescence is considered a natural time of rebellion. But the practice of targeting and meting out of detrimental punishment on poor urban children of color counters the quintessential idea in youth development that in order to grow up to be productive, healthy adults, young people have to be allowed to make mistakes and then be given the opportunity to learn from their transgressions. To learn from one's mistakes requires the resources to do so, and, unfortunately, some young people are not allowed to demonstrate that they are capable of making amends because a vast array of authorities use their transgressions to mark them, minimizing resources for redemption and positive development.

Interactions with authority figures often determine the distribution of resources, as these persons are gatekeepers doling out rewards and punishments. Positive resources may include informal mentoring, choosing not to arrest or incarcerate, referral to youth development, employment training, choosing not to suspend or expel from school, implementing a restorative justice program, affirming young people's desire and ability to utilize positive cultural frames, or creating academic mentoring programs. Negative resources include arrest, humiliation, expulsion from school, stigma, cultural misframing, or placement in a gang database.

Based on these findings, I propose policy and program recommendations. As a researcher, I want to go beyond describing and analyzing the problem to developing possible solutions. While these policy and program recommendations might not change structural conditions and are yet to be tested or perfected, they are insights gathered from years in the field. What practical, day-to-day strategies worked? And can we imagine these strategies being systematically implemented in, say, law-enforcement and educational institutions? Surely, police and schools want to gain insight into how to improve their engagement with marginalized populations and prevent setting up more young people as human targets. Therefore, I offer the following policy and programmatic recommendations.

Cultural Recognition Training

One major policy implication emerging from this study is the need to train school personnel, police and probation officers, and youth workers on how to recognize, interpret, and translate a diverse array of cultural frames. How can authority figures recognize and harness disreputable youths' genuine attempts to be successful within socially acceptable channels? How can these adults' behaviors and attitudes toward youth reinforce these youths' efforts and generate a significant positive impact on their lives?

Young people navigate multiple frames, they have an incredible ability to model shift, and authority figures need to know how to reinforce those frames that are productive and correct those that are misdirected. But adults must be able to understand multiple frames, to read adolescence, and to have enough self-awareness to recognize the implicit and explicit biases that direct typical responses and reactions to specific frames. It is not enough for cultural training to include an understanding of "black culture" or "Latino culture"— as if such universal cultures existed—but, rather, training must include the richness of local community and youth cultures and the particular frames young people encounter as they navigate these multiple, diverse contexts and develop multiple identities accordingly. Cultural understanding at the local community level might include knowing how young people from a specific neighborhood learn to solve their day-to-day adversities. Schools and law enforcement could then incorporate these survival strategies into the messages they deliver to young people and suggest how youths could utilize these unique skills in a conventional setting like a classroom or workplace.

For example, Los Angeles police officer Deon Joseph has been walking the streets of Skid Row in downtown Los Angeles for seventeen years. With experience, he has been able to get to know the people who live in Skid Row, to understand their problems, and to see through what other officers describe as hostility and aggression. He employs community policing to help and to be an agent for change. Offering practical help for desperate people, he believes arrest should always be the last resort. In an interview on National Public Radio, Joseph said, "I'm not stupid or naïve, but I also know if I keep pushing, if they keep looking at me and saying, 'That guy has faith in me. Maybe, maybe, he can guide me to hope.' And that's all I am; all I want to be . . . is a beacon of light in this very, very dark place called Skid Row" (Siegler 2014).

Another officer, "Officer G," as young people refer to him, is a Latino officer in Riverside. He also represents this kind of demeanor. He is well respected by the community, but other officers, as we learned in ride-alongs, see him as the "soft guy," the "community guy," the "hug-a-thug," as "one of them." Instead of officers like Joseph and "G" being exceptions—outcasts and stigmatized in their own departments—they should be the norm. Incentive systems, like promotions and pay increases, should be determined by how police officers engage with community members and by the quality of their interactions.

It is important to develop and implement quality-of-interactions measures in schools and in police departments. These would include personnel evaluations that would take serious input from young people on how educators or police treat them. Teaching evaluations filled out by students might help to provide this kind of information. In the case of police, a website where citizens could rate their interactions with individual officers might provide information to supervisors. We can expect a plethora of unfair negative accounts, but the point is to have information in place that will help us to change the incentive system so that quality of interactions become a top priority for individuals working in systems that play a crucial role in young people's life trajectories.

Understanding other people's cultures as Officer Joseph and Officer "G" do requires emotional intelligence and high-quality interactions. Emotional intelligence is loosely defined as the ability to empathize with others, to recognize emotions, and to use this information to guide thinking and action. Understanding students' emotional well-being allows authority figures to develop practices that students perceive as fair. In turn, perceptions of fairness can shape how individuals react to the enforcement of rules and conduct. In her excellent study on schools and criminal justice, Carla Shedd (2015) found a "carceral continuum" where systems of punishment followed young people across settings and where young people's perceptions of justice and fairness were jeopardize by negative encounters with the system. In this study, I found that the majority of youths did not have a problem following conventional rules and norms, as long as the right incentive systems were in place and as long as they perceived the system as treating them fairly. So if a gang-associated youth encountered a perfect storm of conventional support systems such as a well-paying job, positive interactions with authority figures, and a mentoring relationship with a role model in the community, that youth would be extremely likely to desist from crime and engage in productive activities, including attending school and working.

Likeability is important, too; if young people find that the things they enjoy—like movies, foods, or sports—are also things that authority figures like, it creates the conditions for better connections that, in turn, can improve interactions. How can one treat a friend with disrespect? Of course, friendships are not required here as authority figures have roles to play as educators or enforcers of the law that go beyond the confines of friendship. However, to relate with the young people one engages with brings a deeper connection that allows for better educational and social order opportunities. Getting to know young people minimizes fears that authority figures might have of them. My findings suggest that fear plays a key role in how authority figures treat young people. Fear is a powerful force in our culture, and it is a pillar of the racial divide. When a police officer fears a young Latino or black man, he is more likely to treat him as a severe threat, often ending in harassment or brutality, and sometimes even death. Providing educational programming like ongoing ethnic studies courses to teachers and police provides a context and historical background for these individuals to begin the process of losing their fears of the other.

Incentivize Local Businesses

Some businesses refuse to participate in the criminalization of young people, embracing their presence in the neighborhood and sometimes providing employment opportunities. For me, as a teenager, the auto body shop that provided me my first job gave me an incredible opportunity to manage the turmoil I faced growing up. In Riverland, Abjit of Golden State Liquors afforded the south side boys a modicum of respect and a place to hang out. Taking these examples a step further, public investments could provide subsidies for shop owners like Abjit to hire youths to help keep the store and street corner clean and in order. Such measures would empower Abjit and other well-intentioned business owners to expand their support for marginalized young people and, by extension, their families.

Hire Outreach Workers

School districts should hire outreach workers who can work as cultural translators and cultural educators for both authority figures and youths. Sociologist Patrick Lopez-Aguado (2012) found that street outreach workers—individuals who were former gang members or grew up in rough neighborhoods, acquired higher education, and returned to work with youths in marginalized—developed "street liminality," a position between social worlds. Such caseworkers are in a unique position to navigate multiple contexts and relate within multiple cultural frames to both adults and youths. They are well positioned to teach authority figures how to understand neighborhood youths and to help young people understand the system. They can serve as relevant positive adult role models and healthy examples of gender roles.

As mentors, outreach workers can make a powerful difference in the lives of marginalized young people and counter the fatalistic attitudes that lead to more crime. One goal that outreach workers might have is to help young people see themselves as living longer, more productive lives. By teaching civic engagement, community service, and personal empowerment, the outreach worker might help young people feel empowered to make a change and to improve their communities. Outreach workers should also play the role of advising police and teachers on how to engage and be culturally relevant with marginalized youths. However, their role should be considered one in which they are not required, coerced, or compelled by schools or police to provide information that would set young people up for discipline or punishment.

Invest in Civic Engagement Employment Opportunities

In response to the Great Depression in the 1930s, the federal government invested federal dollars to hire individuals to work in their local communities on projects to benefit the public. One such project, the Civilian Conservation Core (CCC), hired millions of young men to build hundreds of parks, lay miles of roads, and plant millions of trees, among many other projects. The program's benefits included better employment opportunities, elevated morale, and improved health conditions for young working-class men. At the time, some believed that the CCC was building roads to nowhere, but many of these roads now provide access to national and state parks and serve as commuting routes throughout the United States. The benefits to millions of young men were tremendous, and no one today seriously questions the value of the CCC program or its accomplishments.

Similarly, the odds are stacked against populations in many inner cities with high rates of unemployment, victimization, crime, and incarceration. A program at the scale of the CCC, combined with programming to help individuals acquire trade and academic credentials, could increase educational attainment, job security, and crime desistance among gang-associated and at-promise youths. A system of opportunities and skills training could strengthen those cultural frames that call for hard work while enabling a new generation of young people access to mainstream success.

Father Greg Boyle, a renowned Jesuit priest and gang outreach worker in Los Angeles, shares his mantra on violence prevention: "Nothing stops a bullet like a job." His program, Homeboy Industries, is world renowned for transforming gang-associated individuals. One of his central strategies is to find employment for his clients, and Father Boyle has persuaded many local companies to hire individuals with prison records and facial tattoos but who are committed to changing their lives. Homeboy Industries operates a bakery and several restaurants—including the Homegirl Café in one of the Los Angeles International Airport terminals—that employ those who have been rejected by other employers because of their criminal records, tattoos, or *cholo* demeanor. Having a job creates a sense of belonging, hope, opportunity, self-reliance, and transformation. In short, jobs change lives, prevent further descent into a criminal lifestyle, and satisfy a basic yearning many youths express: simply to be given a chance, to feel a sense of purpose and belonging.

Although an exemplary model, Homeboy Industries relies mainly on revenue from its businesses, soft monies, grants, and private donations. We also need local, state, and federal governments to invest consistent monies in creating and sustaining programs similar to Homeboy Industries and the once-successful CCC. In the latter model, clients worked in public service and public works initiatives that provided them an opportunity to have a purpose as they helped their communities. Hand in hand, both models could synergize a national program for employment and life skills. Short-term investments would be well met in the long-term as dollars spent on imprisoning people shifted to a civic and social good. In the words of artist and political activist Mike de la Rocha, "we need a new, new deal" for marginalized urban communities.

Invest in Educational and Legal Fairness

When individuals believe institutions like schools and the legal system have treated them unjustly, they are more likely to scoff at the rules, or at least appear to do so. For example, research in procedural justice has affirmed that when citizens perceived that police-citizen interactions were fair, they viewed the police as legitimate, which influenced how the police were received. Similarly, education research has shown that Latinos' perceptions of fairness and justice in schools impacted their academic achievement. What if institutions invested in improving perceptions of fairness? This might lead young people to believe that they had a chance to make it through the system and, therefore, to become invested in completing their program within the system—whether a probation plan or a high school degree.

But gaining legitimacy with marginalized populations must not be the end goal for schools and police departments. This step is just the beginning. It is after gaining trust that the real work begins—the work of generating and facilitating positive resources, symbolic and material, so that viable opportunities open up. Authority figures must connect with the populations they work with while finding creative strategies for implementing policies and programs that bring about resources that help to promote more sustainable livelihoods. Recognizing and accepting young people's multiply complex selves is a first step in helping marginalized youths contend with adversity. Providing them resources and reflecting on how we treat them, and assessing how fear of the other plays a role in our everyday interactions, are essential in this process. In order to help people not only to survive but also to thrive, institutions must restore their dignity, provide viable resources, recognize and work with their full human complexity, and dismantle punitive policies and practices. Crime, violence, police brutality, and school failure all seem like unsolvable social issues. However, with enough human recognition, with treating marginalized young people as if they are our own children, with stripping away from schools and law enforcement the permission to treat racialized, criminalized youths as less than human or less than white humans, we will expand the possibility to eliminate the system that creates human targets and instead propagate a system—a youth support complex—that promotes human well-being across institutional settings.

METHODOLOGICAL APPENDIX

The data for this study comes from five years of extensive observations on street corners, at a continuation high school, at a conventional high school, in courtrooms, at a community center, and during police ride-alongs. In addition, I supervised 218 in-depth, semi-structured interviews with fifty-seven males and twelve females and thirty-four focus group sessions. I hired a team of graduate and undergraduate research assistants to help run the focus groups and interviews; they conducted 102 of the 218 interviews. While a few of the students conducted informal observations and took field notes, primarily at school sites and at the community center, unless otherwise noted in specific chapters, the observational data reported in this book come from my own fieldwork.

We held focus group interviews at a community center in their neighborhood where they would be welcomed and not subject to the stigmatization they expressed feeling in many public spaces. This technique also allowed us to keep close tabs on a population that is difficult to track down in the field. I went to them whenever possible, but in case I could not reach them, I created a regular time and place that remained consistent for over a four-year period, even during holidays, where they knew they could show up and check in. I also met up with these youths regularly throughout the week in the street or at local parks in their neighborhood. These more informal meetings were useful for collecting observations and personal narratives, but also helped me build rapport with the youth and recruit them for the weekly focus groups at the community center.

My three-fold methodology—observations, focus groups, and interviews—facilitated multiple perspectives in the research process, allowing for comparisons and disconfirming evidence. Focus groups helped me develop and test interview questions and provided different insight from individual interviews. In-depth interviews brought out information not available through any other methodological medium. I did not take participants' testimonies for granted but instead used them to understand their worldviews and to compare with other data collected. For the observation component, I "shadowed" young people to gain an understanding of the social processes they experienced through daily routines. The "shadow" approach allows the researcher to follow people as they navigate their daily lives (Rios 2011). This research strategy allows the researcher to observe young people across social contexts. This may be one of the solutions to a major gap in gang studies: the need for studying gang members as they navigate various institutions (Coughlin and Venkatesh 2003). Remaining static on a street corner or inside the walls of institutions will not elicit the content of social processes that we need to uncover in order to understand gang association. A social process is understood here as the "transactions between two or more people or groups of people in a setting" (Tseng and Siedman 2007). Close observation and interaction uncover a unique dimension of settings and social processes. Shadowing allowed me access to their routine activities within their various social networks and reference groups. It also allowed me to see how their activities and ways of being in the world shifted in different social settings (e.g., on the corner with friends or in school). This became a crucial approach as I attempted to uncover the multiple frames at work in the lives of these young people. I used place and setting as sampling frames and as critical analytic frames—à la grounded theory (Glaser and Strauss 1967; Charmaz 2002a, 2002b). That is, I compared differential behavioral patterns and experiential perceptions in the different settings that youths navigated.

Studying Cultural Frames in Participants

The research participants were gang-associated youths from Riverland, California, a city with an approximately 70 percent white, primarily upper-middle-class population and an approximately

30 percent Latino, primarily working-class population, located in Southern California.[1] The neighborhood where this study was conducted is located in a census tract with a median household income of $26,000 per year and a majority Latino population. By contrast, an adjacent census tract with a majority white population hosts a median household income of $112,000 per year. This close proximity economic disparity offers the researcher an opportunity to analyze how working-class Latino youths understand themselves and their social worlds in a context with vast economic disparities between two racial groups.

I recruited participants through purposive, snowball sampling, by which I made contact with a small group and then asked this group to introduce me to and network me with other youths from the neighborhood. I used grounded theory to uncover common themes and patterns that developed and searched for unique cases (Strauss 1987).

Because of the risk of being identified as a probation or police officer or snitch on the street when taking field notes on a notepad, I took notes after I returned home from my observations. Whenever pertinent events occurred whereby I wanted to recall exact excerpts from the field, I utilized a cell-phone technique where I stepped a few feet away from participants and texted myself notes and quotes, or used a notes application on my phone, in order to protect the integrity of the data (see Goffman 2009). I analyzed field notes, interviews, and focus group transcripts by coding in Dedoose, a mixed-methods software program. I utilized "focused coding" to generate dominant themes and eliminate inconsistent findings (Emerson, Fretz, and Shaw 1995). I used Payne's insight (2006) that while the experiences of street-life-oriented youth who are recruited through snowball sampling are not representative, their perspectives "provide an understanding for how the streets operate as a site for economic, social, and psychological grounding of masculinity." I also utilized Young's (2006) "worldview perspective." Young analyzes the perspectives of black men as active agents making choices and negotiating the social and economic forces attempting to weaken them, rather than as just "passive reactors" waiting to be victimized by the system (2006, 5). Every move, every action, reflects their ability to critically react to their situations. They are more than just "violent-prone individuals who mindlessly lash out at the world with hostility and aggression"; they are complex individuals negotiating barriers and exploring opportunities in the world around them (Young 2006, 5).

Like Young's participants, Latino youth in this study actively created a range of worldviews, comprised of their beliefs and thoughts, which helped them to assign meaning to their social worlds (Young 2006; see also Geertz 1973 and Harding 2010). This worldview perspective is a move away from using values and norms as frameworks for explaining individual behavior and aims; rather, this approach explores how patterns of thought become "common sense" for individuals and how individuals engage in critical and creative reflections about their lives and future prospects. One's worldview, or system of meaning-making, constitutes a basis for future behavior (Geertz 1973). Individual worldviews are a composite of frames based on whatever place individuals navigate to in the social world and their subsequent actions within this world. Young asserts that the way people think about the processes of social and personal mobility is important, as it "informs us about how they choose to act" (Young 2006, 11). Beliefs are the "cultural fabric" that inform and encourage people's behavior. I used Giddens's (1979, 1984) insight that social structures and people's actions often operate simultaneously; we act out our social lives within a "duality of structure" (1984, 379).

This approach contributes to the cultural turn in ethnography— exemplified by scholars like David Harding, Mario Small, Alford Young, Michelle Lamont, and Natasha Warikoo—where culture is examined beyond "values" and "codes," brought front and center (without "blaming the victim"), and examined as fluid and dynamic. Ultimately, I find that culture is crucial, that the quality of interactions determines worldviews and outcomes among young people, and that those subcultures created by young people that authority figures deem as negative can be dynamic and adapted to positive outcomes, such as success in school and the labor market, when positive interactions with authority figures are placed into practice.

Studying the Gang

Most gang studies to date have neglected to examine gangs across institutional settings (Coughlin and Venkatesh 2003; exceptions include Decker and Van Winkle [1996] and Esbensen et al. [1993]) and distinguish between gang crime and youthful collective behavior (Sullivan 2005). The literature on gangs shows us that youth involved in gangs are more likely to commit crime, become incarcerated, and be victimized (Esbensen and Huizinga 1993; Vigil 2010; Klein and Maxson 2010). Much of the sociological literature on gangs is concerned with understanding why young people join gangs and commit gang violence, as well as how gangs become entrepreneurial (Coughlin and Venkatesh 2003; Klein and Maxson 2010). I wanted to move beyond examining these themes and attempt to uncover the role that social settings, specifically interaction with peers and authority figures—school personnel and law enforcement—played in the lives of youths who had been labeled as gang members by law enforcement.

Vigil (1988) and Hagedorn (1988) have found that conflict with authority figures influences gang involvement. Other scholars have found that high commitment to delinquent peers and low commitment to positive peers also influences gang involvement (Esbensen and Huizinga 1993; Vigil 1988). Vigil (1988) has found that gang-associated young men develop *locura*—performing dangerous, courageous, bravado behaviors—in order to cope with adversity. This *locura* may develop from a lack of positive interactions with family, school, and peers (Esbensen et al. 1993) or negative labeling by teachers (Esbensen and Huzinga 1993). In order to make up for negative relations with mainstream institutions, gang-associated youths may search for belonging, protection, and self-esteem in the gang-associated group (Curry and Spergel 1992; Fagan 1990; Horowitz

1983). Panel studies have found that detachment from social control institutions—parents and teachers—lead to gang involvement because young people have low levels of social integration (Thornberry 1998). However, most panel studies on gangs miss social processes and social settings. While panel studies have a lot to teach us about the demography and attitudes of gang members, they are not able to provide an in-depth understanding of the social processes that shape the lives of gang-associated youths. This study sought to complement these studies by demonstrating how social settings impact decision making, cultural frames, and outcomes for young people.

Gaining Entrée

The issue of entrée needs highlighting because it may be the researcher's biggest obstacle. I began looking for gang-associated youths by contacting the principal at one of the local continuation high schools, Punta Vista. I told the principal that I wanted to work with a group of students who she or the community believed were at-risk and gang-associated. I told her I wanted to study a group of gang-associated youths and that I was willing to establish a mentoring program and a series of workshops focused on higher education and careers for a small group of these participants. The principal was intrigued by the idea that some of her students could be helped by my students. Eventually, twelve of my undergraduate students became mentors for her students; my graduate students assisted in developing and running a once-a-week community college workshop that enrolled eighteen students in the local community college. These students reported that they would never have considered going to the community college if it hadn't been for the program. The principal told me that in the past five years, only two or three of her students enrolled in the community college each year. None of these students ended up becoming part of the research project. This additional project was a means for me to help out students at the school while gaining access.

The principal introduced me to a group of twenty students. After spending some time observing their class, I presented my study to them and asked for volunteers; four young men showed interest. These youths met me after school at the local community center located a few blocks away. I provide each of them ten dollars for each interview. I then asked them to refer me to other youths. After a handful of interviews and repeated contacts, my students and I gained enough trust from this group to get invited to "the hangout spot." "If you want the homies, you gotta go to them," Mario, one of our informants, told us. This is when I began the process of shadowing youths, following them across settings and recruiting more participants as I became embedded in each setting.

Over time, I became curious about police perceptions of the boys in the study. I asked the boys their thoughts on me riding along with police. Most of them were indifferent, but a few cautioned me about being seen by the homies as a snitch should they see me inside a patrol car. Therefore, I waited until I left the streets and community center field sites to conduct ride-alongs with police, four years into the study. I hired a graduate student who had not had contact with any of the boys in the past to help me conduct these ride-alongs. This way I could compare my field notes with him to see what kind of bias lens I had developed from my time on the streets and to ensure that I did not influence the observations should police officers encounter boys from the study while I was in the patrol car. We asked the chief of police permission to conduct ride-alongs. He agreed and connected us with one of his sergeants to coordinate a schedule. We conducted a combined thirty-two ride-alongs with police officers, where we observed forty-six police encounters with Latino gang-associated youths.

There were many times when I lost track of the goal of this study. Moments where, for instance, I developed a deep resentment and anger toward some of the boys, educators, or officers in the study. During the write-up of this book, I read about these instances in my field notes, and I recalled my feelings at the time. I believe that these feelings had an influence on the organization, writing style, and framework presented in this book. Also, my own experience and preconceived understanding of what was happening in the field, that young people were being criminalized and dehumanized, played a role in the development of this project. I can't claim to not have a bias, as all social scientists undertake their research enterprise with partiality, even if they uncritically claim objectivity. My goal here was to present a nuanced perspective of the lives and processes that the young people I studied encountered. I reviewed my analysis and write-up several times to check for typologizing discourse or descriptions that would make young people appear one-dimensional or caricaturized. While no amount of writing can accurately represent a true-to-life account, instead of aiming for authenticity, I aimed for complexity. I figured that if I gave an account of the multiple selves that one encounters in the field, both from subjects and from subjectivity, I would be a step closer in providing a glimpse into how the nexus between institutions and individuals is mediated by complex personhoods. This way I could defy the problematic literature on the poor that makes them appear trapped in a one-dimensional world with one-dimensional identities.

Moving beyond the White Space in Urban Ethnography

In recent years, ethnography has experienced a resurgence in urban sociology. Urban sociology was founded by the Chicago school, which placed a strong emphasis on conducting research on the ground. However, ethnographic work in sociology became marginalized in the discipline during its conservative decades in the late twentieth century (circa 1950s–1980s). In the 1990s, we saw a renaissance of work that emphasized grounded research uncovering the firsthand data collection of urban life (e.g., Anderson 1990, 1999; Duneier 1992, 1999; Newman 1999; Patillo-McCoy 1999). Examining how people make sense of their situated realities and how conditions and processes unravel in real time has become more and more a theme of study for urban sociologists. Sociology departments across the country continue to hire scholars conducting this kind of work, and more students of sociology are turning to ethnography as a field of training.

But despite being considered a critical, modish, reflexive sub-discipline, urban sociology is plagued with issues. These include a hypermasculine, heteronormative gaze (for an exception, see Pascoe 2007); a neoliberal pandering to the masses (see Wacquant's infamous critique (2002); and a personal-narrative-promoting platform for eccentric scholars (see, e.g., Goffman 2014; Rios 2011; Venkatesh 2008). In my assessment, the most pressing issue in urban ethnography today (and in sociology writ large) is "the white space."

Elijah Anderson (2015) defines the white space as the "over-whelmingly white neighborhoods, restaurants, schools, universities, workplaces, churches and other associations, courthouses, and cemeteries, a situation that reinforces a normative sensibility in settings in which black people are typically absent, not expected, or marginalized when present"(10). Anderson explains that "white spaces vary in kind, but their most visible and distinctive feature is their overwhelming presence of white people and their absence of black people" (13). The most conspicuous component of this white space is that its

> racism is more commonly manifested in a pervasive attitude that all black people start from the inner-city ghetto, and before experiencing decent treatment or trusting relations with others, they must demonstrate that the ghetto stereotype does not apply to them. Despite positive social change and the growth of the black middle class, it is still the case that when encountering blacks in the white space, some whites experience cognitive dissonance and, if for no other reason than the need to set the dissonant picture straight, become confused or disturbed, or even outraged at what they see. . . . In the

interest of consonance, they try to put the black person "back in his place"—at times telling him in no uncertain terms to "go back where you came from." (14)

Let's introduce Anderson's notion of the white space to the practice of urban sociology. Racism is created and perpetuated by everyone in society, including sociologists. A component of racism, as described by Anderson, is to put people in their racialized place. What if the work of ethnographers has been to put the "other" that we study back in its place? What if we have had the limited reflexivity to develop accounts that go beyond typecasting/racializing the populations we study? What if we have been cognitively trapped in the white space? The white space in urban ethnography is that amalgamation of works that have perpetuated stereotypes of marginalized populations and even created new racialized understandings of these populations (such as the notion that hardened criminals represent the entire overpoliced population and therefore making entire inner-city populations require such harsh policing). The white space is also a social-psychological state of being in that our attitudes, perceptions, and cultural frames operate to conduct work that perpetuates whiteness, white privilege, and white spaces. And we don't even know it. Anthropologist John Hartigan (1999) asks a crucial question about social science research: "How are we to effect a change in Americans' tendency to view social life through a lens of 'black and white' when we rely upon and reproduce the same categories in our analyses and critiques of the way race matters in this country?" (3).

This white space is often invisible to the researcher (an important reason why a consistent reflexive approach must be implemented in all stages of the research process—including in the writing stage, a step often ignored). It is the white space that allows even the most well-meaning sociologists to create a logic trap for themselves by making the essence of their work a project of normalizing and humanizing the other. At best, the end result is sometimes a pandering to mass (white) audiences in an attempt to normalize foreign worlds (people of color). Duneier et al. explain in "The Urban Ethnography Reader" (2014): "We hope readers will also agree that this literature [the canon of urban ethnography] clarifies patient, skilled and hard-working observers can render individuals of *other* than their own *race, class, gender* and circumstances recognizable and understandable" (5; emphasis mine). At first glance, this excerpt appears to assume that researchers are all homogenous (white) and that we are all studying an "other." Urban ethnography should not be about making the strange familiar; it should be about making the familiar strange. It should be about bringing out the human complexity that exists in all the populations we study across the stratification spectrum. We have to create an urban ethnography that is more embracive of multiple perspectives, that is comfortable with a cadre of ethnographers that persistently questions our intentions and our role as researchers. The only way to accomplish this is through a thorough and decolonial reflexivity of the white space (see Tuhiwai-Smith [1999] for a brilliant practical example for doing so). James Clifford reminds us that ethnography is allegory (1986). It becomes a multidimensional symbol that represents a momentary lived reality, a homogenous interpretation of culture, and the ethnographers own worldview:

> A recognition of allegory emphasizes the fact that realistic portraits, to the extent that they are "convincing" or "rich," are extended metaphors, patterns of associations that point to coherent (theoretical, esthetic, moral) additional meanings. . . . Allegory draws special attention to the *narrative* character of cultural representations, to the stories built into the representational process itself. One level of meaning in a text will always generate other levels. . . . What one *sees* in a coherent ethnographic account, the imaged construct of the other, is connected in a continuous double structure with what one *understands*. (100, 101)

To recognize how we participate in the construction of symbols that represent a particular reality at a particular temporality through a particular epistemology and standpoint is to begin the work of re-flexivity. But the white space often gets in the way of this process. At worst, the (heteronormative, hypermasculine, neoliberal) white space makes us blind to our various privileges and places us at the center of the universe that we are studying; our subjects simply re-volve around us. The white space sometimes produces a *Lawrence of Arabia* syndrome in some scholars, where we not only become the native, but our own fantasized manifestation of the native—a warped sense of the native's reality seen through the prism of the white space—and utilize this unreflexive reality as a social program to speak for the masses, not with them. In order to correct the false logic that the white space is producing, we have to provide adequate mentoring to younger generations of scholars. But how can we do so if many of those mentoring new ethnographers are, not only epis-temologically centered in the white space, but also staunch propo-nents of the white space?

For those sociologists that argue that this kind of critique is against white people conducting research on populations of color or that scholars of color are exempt from the white space, think again. The white space is embedded in all of us. We are colonized by it. As such, in order to address it in our work, we have to maintain a con-sistent, overzealous reflexivity. One where we constantly ask our-selves about our research design, our relationship with our research participants, the labels we give them, and the way we write about them. True, it is critical that we strive to provide an authentic per-spective of what we observe. But isn't authenticity fully complex? Aren't humans from all walks of life complicated and heteroge-neous in their values, culture, and actions? (See Hannerz 2004 and Patillo-McCoy 1999.) If so, why is it that we continue to write about poor populations as if they were cartoon characters, for example, as "clean" or "dirty"?

Some colleagues have approached me about my critiques of Alice Goffman's recent high-profile book *On the Run* (see Rios 2015a) and have asked questions like, "Do you think that people are being harsh on that scholar because she is white?" To which I have replied with a question, "Have you read Jamie Fader's book, *Falling Back*?" In 2013, Jamie Fader published a book on urban young men from Philadelphia that were caught up in the criminal justice system. She followed them across multiple institutional settings over three years to understand them in their full complexity, as students, wards, streetlife participants, fathers, and workers. This book was exceptionally reflexive, ethnographically rich, and theoretically compelling. It is as if it had been written with deep awareness of the white space. Fader made it a point to discuss how race played out in her encounters with the young men in the book, how her privileges impacted her gaze, and to capture larger structural forces at play when writing about the intricate complexities of the lives of the young men in her study. Many of the colleagues that I had conversations with regarding recent developments in ethnography didn't even know this book existed. I then asked them, "Did you know that Jamie Fader is white?"

Another scholar whose work exemplifies deep reflexivity and a genuine attempt at preventing the caricaturization of the poor is Matt Desmond (2016). Desmond reflects on his experience as a white ethnographer,

> But the truth is that white people are afforded special privileges in the ghetto. For one, my interactions with the police were nonintrusive and quick, even after a pair of separate shootings happened outside my front door . . . a white person living in and writing about the inner city is not uniquely exposed to threats but uniquely shielded from them . . . people often started cleaning up and apologizing after meeting me for the first time. In my late twenties, I was called "sir" countless more times than I was told by some young tough to get a "G pass"—a "gangster pass," essentially to account for my white self. (322)

He attempts to eliminate himself from the center of the story and instead focuses on the deep multidimensional complexity of the people he studies. His approach throughout the text is to understand

and illustrate that while people he studies are broke, they are not broken—"Poverty has not prevailed against their deep humanity" (335). More approaches like Fader's and Desmond's must be developed in order to reverse the pathologizing effects of other ethnographies focused on the poor.

Urban ethnography requires a decolonization of the white space. Urban ethnographers, like other sociologists, have secured career benefits from studying marginalized populations, held a stake in knowledge production about the urban poor, and even provided the language and discourse for the state to perpetuate race and class domination. While many ethnographers have discussed their positionality relative to the marginalized populations they study, very few have implemented a system of checks and balances in their work that questions whether their own whiteness, or their support for a system of whiteness, has compromised the knowledge-production process. Even fewer have reflected on the system of whiteness that has made them into experts of ghettoized "others." On the contrary, whiteness has been a coveted, euphemistic characteristic if a researcher is to be considered objective and a great researcher and writer. A reflexivity of whiteness calls for all researchers to reflect on how their identity and color blindness might be whitewashing the research process and, in turn, tainting the knowledge-production process—creating one-dimensional caricaturized images of the urban "other" and limiting our ability to systematically understand the populations we study. Mario Luis Small (2015, 356) cautions us that as researchers we have the power to exploit the populations we study: "when an ethnographer either purposely or unwittingly improves her representation of herself by worsening the representation of the observed, she risks a kind of rhetorical exploitation." One question to ask ourselves as we conduct our research and writing is, am I participating in the process of making myself look better than the subjects I have studied?

Moving forward, we should strive to develop multiple forms of knowledge from multiple vantage points about the multiple realities that our participants live and experience; reflect critically on our privileges as knowledge producers, narrators, and theory creators; and develop research with a purpose that is translational and aims to improve the conditions of the populations we study, without perpetuating a neoliberal savior complex. This, of course, is easier said than done. As such, the methods in this book were just that—an *attempt* at decolonizing the white space that inhabits my own work.

ACKNOWLEDGMENTS

I am deeply grateful for the people that helped to make this book a reality. First and foremost, I am thankful to the young people in this book that opened their lives up and trusted me with their stories and experiences. My collaborator, best friend, wife, and coparent, Rebeca Mireles-Rios, has been an incredible supporter of my work. She found superhuman ways for completing a doctorate degree and raising three children while I got lost in the field for what seemed to her an eternity, and when I finally returned, she patiently helped me work through the heavy experiences I encountered. Thank you, Beba. Anonymous reviewers at the University of Chicago Press saw promise in this research project early on. The William T. Grant Foundation provided generous funding for the completion of this project. Countless undergraduate students, too numerous to name here, helped to collect, transcribe, and code focus group data. They formed a powerful, supportive, and insightful research collective, self-described as the "Rios Dream Team." Three of these under-graduate students helped to manage this research team over the years: Elsa Hernandez, Jose Lumbreras, and Amy Martinez. Many graduate students also participated in the focus group and inter-view data–collection process. These include Jerry Flores, Francisco Fuentes, Mario Galicia, Melissa Guzman, Patrick Lopez-Aguado, Gisselle Lopez-Tello, Greg Prieto, Cesar Rodriguez, and Rachel Sarabia. These students were instrumental in helping me develop, test, and troubleshoot ideas. Community members who worked directly with the youths were amazing supporters providing me with a space to meet with on a weekly basis, with initial contact, and with services for youths in need; they included Raquel L. and Ismael H. My good friend Cid Martinez took the time to read chapters and provide feedback as the book unfolded. Chandra Russo and Salvador

Rangel helped me find relevant theories and literature to bolster my ideas. The Racial Democracy, Crime and Justice Network, at the time led by Ruth Peterson and Laurie Krivo, was an instrumental group of supportive and rigorous colleagues who helped me develop my larger intellectual agenda. Other colleagues and friends provided me formal and informal feedback as well—you know who you are, and I expect you to remind me so that I can apologize for forgetting to acknowledge you.

NOTES

INTRODUCTION

1. A note to reader: these events occurred over twenty years ago. While I remember some conversations vividly, I have done my best to represent these experiences to the best of my recollection. Some of the direct quotes in this introduction are different than the empirical, direct quotes from recordings or field notes in the chapters that follow—actual, recorded accounts. The quotes regarding my experience as a teenager are quotes created from my memory of these events.

2. See Andrea Boyle's (2016) exemplary book for detailed accounts of how black Americans experience policing based on race and community context.

3. Forest Stuart's (2016) brilliant book describes a process by which police often have positive intent but end up treating marginalized, homeless populations extremely negatively because of the institutional factors that inhibit human connection.

4. See Vigil (1988, 2002) for a framework explaining the multiple levels of identity among gang-associated youths.

5. The use of diametrically opposed categories is a fallacy long recognized in urban ethnography. Ulf Hannerz (2004) addressed this dilemma in his classic study: "The simple dichotomy seems often to emerge from social science writing, about poor black people or the lower class . . . perhaps because the observers have simply accepted the moral taxonomy of the natives as an acceptable way of ordering descriptions of the community, or because a similar dichotomy fits the outsider's moral precepts or his concern for social problems."

6. Such an argument builds on a rich lineage of social research that finds import in the notion of "identity work," that is, how social actors perform different iterations of the self in accordance with situational context. Sociologists have long suggested the conceptual category of identity, if often ambiguous, can offer a theoretically meaningful lynchpin for understanding the relationship between self and society, a key concern of the sociological discipline. By examining the identity work of at-risk youths, we gain a more

nuanced understanding of both the institutions they navigate and the behaviors they adopt. See Snow and Anderson (1987).

7. See Vigil (2007, chap. 2), on the mixed methods of gang research. The
term "triangulation" originates with the notion of using three points to situ-
ate oneself on a geographical map. In qualitative sociological studies, triangulation is not dissimilar and is used as an important means for assur-
ing a study's validity across different contexts. When I use the term, I draw
on Denzin's concept of data triangulation that uses data to examine a phenomenon in several different settings and different points in time or space
(Denzin 1970). Simply speaking, through reliance on three or more different data sources, I am able to juxtapose my sources of information to ensure
my claims are empirically sound and reasonably generalizable. In addition,
triangulation of data is key to my theoretical point: Only by observing gang-
associated youth across distinct times and institutional spaces can we grasp
how these social actors are able to shift to meet various social arrangements
they confront.

8. http://www.vera.org/files/price-of-prisons-california-fact-sheet.pdf.

9. For a thorough and powerful study of Latina girls caught up in the
juvenile justice system, see my former student Jerry Flores's 2016 book,
Caught Up: Girls, Surveillance, and Wraparound Incarceration.

10. John Eason's (2016) compelling ethnography on prisons demonstrates how racial violence and stigma help to obfuscate the damaging outcomes of prisonization and prison building. Collective memory built on
racial resentment and fogged by racial indifference serves to hide the harsh
realities of the punitive state from everyday people that might otherwise
care. In this same manner, racial violence and stigma help to cover up the
severe damages that harsh school discipline and punitive policing have on
marginalized young people.

11. A burgeoning food justice movement has gentrified some local food
production and distribution sites. A few scholars have explored instances in
which farmers' markets have come to operate as spaces for whites, despite
many vendors being people of color. For one insightful, comparative ethnographic account of California markets, see Alkon and McCullen (2010).

12. The understanding that race and class along with other categories
of social experience are co-constituted and intersect to shape people's lives
is almost taken for granted in sociology and across disciplines (Collins
1998; Crenshaw 1991; Hooks 1984). Adding considerations of age, particular regional racial histories, and state policies regarding migration make an
"intersectional analysis" particularly salient for this project.

13. Criminologist Jody Miller (1995) argued that police determine cul-

pability based on the performance of gangster style. She contended, "Style has become a vehicle through which social control agents interact with gang members" (214). The more "gangster" a young person looks or acts, the more likely police and probation are to punish them.

14. Alice Goffman, in her polemic 2014 book *On the Run*, could have used the "gang" label for her research participants. However, she avoided this pitfall by avoiding previous scholars' loose definition of gangs.

15. Scholars across various disciplines remind us that the cultural constructs and linguistic tools we use to understand people's behaviors and to characterize whole populations are neither strictly psychological nor abstract, but have concrete ramifications in institutions, policies, and people's lives. In addition, a variety of studies point to the vicious cycle established when communities are defined in particular ways and their treatment institutionalized accordingly (see Schneider and Igraham 1993). I elaborate further on this in my discussion of labeling theory.

16. Nicole Gonzalez Van Cleeve's (2015) groundbreaking book demonstrates how poor racialized populations are mistreated and unjustly criminalized in the court system. Many of my observations in courtrooms confirm Gozalez Van Cleeve's findings—the court system serves as a system of racialized punitive social control.

17. Criminologists and practitioners continue to vehemently debate whether aggressively punitive deterrence strategies actually prevent crime. Wilson and Kelling (1982) suggested in their now classic (and highly controversial) broken windows theory that the more intensively urban environments are policed and even petty crime is punished, the greater public safety will be. A number of scholars contest this notion (Garland 2001; Kennedy 2009), suggesting that many punitive crime prevention strategies actually facilitate greater criminality.

18. A central tenant in the sociological canon is the idea that what and whom society labels as deviant has wide-ranging consequences. Often termed "labeling theory," sociologists have suggested that not only do individuals come to understand themselves and their identities by the labels that society gives them, but that the social-psychological consequences of such labeling can influence behavior. The notion emerged from the work of Émile Durkheim, who considered criminal activity not so much an empirical given, but a category of action that when labeled deviant is functional to society's desire for general order and control. Edwin Lemert (1951) built on this idea to theorize two kinds of deviance: primary and secondary. The former is the actual criminal behavior, and the latter includes the host of explanations and lived behaviors that an individual ultimately enacts to iden-

tify as deviant. Becker (1963) developed these ideas further through empirical work on marijuana users and musicians.

19. Rather than the idea that culture offers a set of ultimate end values that influence individuals' actions, Swidler (1986) argued that toolkits or "repertoires" of "habits, skills, and styles" are a better representation of how people decide to do what they do. Rather than select their actions one by one, individuals as social beings are more likely to pull from a relatively constrained set of recognizable, patterned, and culturally meaningful behaviors.

20. Social thinkers have suggested that society's marginalized may be better equipped to recognize social structures than their more privileged counterparts, and therefore, to navigate the various cultural frames existent in a given time and place. Although not explicitly concerned with culture, sociologist W. E. B. DuBois (1903) nevertheless offered some foundational thinking on this matter when he argued that African Americans were forced to understand their social positions from various purviews, thus seeing multiply ("the veil") and maintaining the cognitive dissonance of multiple cultural frames ("double consciousness"). Feminist theorists also have suggested that those who experience oppression have a perspective on society—a marginalized standpoint—that might allow them a better view of how power works in their social milieu (Hartsock 1983). Finally, bringing these ideas together, black feminist sociologist Patricia Hill Collins (1986, 15) argued that black women's "outsider within status" provides a set of marginal standpoints that can offer creative potential and intellectual rigor, and that these "standpoints promise to enrich contemporary sociological discourse" itself. See also Young (2004), Harding (2010) and Small et al. (2010).

21. See my critique of Alice Goffman (Rios 2015a) and my paper on the white space in urban ethnography (2015b).

22. Although recent studies concerning gangs have not analyzed this process, classic studies were very focused in this arena; see MacKlein's *Street Gangs and Street Workers* (1971) and Short and Strodtbeck's *Group Process and Gang Delinquency* (1965).

CHAPTER ONE

1. In the snowball sampling method, existing research participants suggest other members of their social network as potentially appropriate participants. Although this method cannot provide a representative sample of a given population (gang-affiliated youth, in this instance), it is a widely recognized appropriate means for collecting qualitative data among com-

munity members who might otherwise be difficult to locate or enlist to participate in a research study. See Babbie 2001.

2. For an excellent historical account of the development of the *Californio* identity construction, see Sanchez (1995).

3. Mark's expression here was well theorized in his identification with, not only a historically marginalized ethnic group, but also an indigenous one, the Chumash. At the basic level, he located himself in a kind of identity politics. (See Bernstein and Taylor's definition of identity politics in *The Wiley-Blackwell Encyclopedia of Social and Political Movements* [2013]). Alfred and Corntassel (2005) also suggested that maintaining indigenous identification in the face of state and market forces, what they term an "imperial institutional network," can be understood as an alternative to "dispossession and disconnection" in the contemporary sociopolitical order.

4. A good deal of research suggests that youth of color are less likely than their white counterparts to receive adequate care for ADHD, which is today the most commonly diagnosed mental health disorder in children. For instance, Morgan et al. (2013) noted that "racial/ethnic minorities have been reported to be diagnosed with ADHD at lower rates than white children, and therefore may have unmet treatment needs" (86).

5. A study surveying three different nationwide data sets found that "of children and adolescents six to seventeen years old who were defined as needing mental health services, nearly eighty percent did not receive mental health care" (Kataoka, Zhang, and Wells 2002)

6. The majority of the thirty-six to forty-three arrests I witnessed during a four-year period were for probation violations. Those persons on probation must follow specific rules during the probationary period, which include actively working or going to school and avoiding known gang members, alcohol and drugs, and specific locations.

7. A major mistake committed by some researchers that study marginalized populations is that they take for granted that these people have single dominant identities and label them with fixed categories. Often times, this is a result of taking folk categories at face value (see Hannerz [2004] for a conversation of this fallacy and Goffman [2014] for an example of the mistake).

8. A range of literatures indicates that young people growing up in poverty are exposed to a variety of factors that risk their mental health. Although many of these are social factors—chaotic living situations, weak support networks, neighborhood violence, and few public services—the impact of air and water pollution must be considered as part of the puzzle.

Gary W. Evans (2004) suggested, "The accumulation of multiple environmental risks rather than a singular risk of exposure may be an especially pathogenic aspect of childhood poverty."

9. See the methodological appendix for details on gaining entrée to the school and other field sites.

10. Michel Foucault (1977) long ago argued that the school and prison had come to resemble each other under a novel regime of disciplinarity. The school and the prison, he suggested, along with factories, hospitals, and army barracks constitute "complete and austere institutions," meaning that people spend a good deal of their time together in such places, sequestered from the larger society and abiding by a highly regimented and routinized daily existence. In more contemporary work, scholars have built on this basic notion to theorize that the school is an extension of a massive carceral apparatus that exists to manage and contain surplus populations the world over (Giroux 2013; Robinson and Barrera 2012; Wacquant 2009). Other more quantitative studies have empirically verified the links between race, poverty, and exclusionary school security measures (Kupchik and Ward 2014).

11. A few scholars have examined the construction of gender identities among men caught up in the various institutional cultures of the criminal justice system (Sabo et. al 2001). Pascoe's (2011) ethnography on high school students also offers a compelling portrait of the intertwining of homophobia and the constructions of masculinity. See chapter 4 for a more rigorous analysis of gender.

12. As I theorized on the social bond forged within the gang, I returned in many ways to the founding sociological thinkers—Durkheim, Marx, Weber—who all were centrally preoccupied with the cultivation of solidarity in the face of modernity's dramatic economic, political, and social upheavals. Now, under a neoliberal global order that has created new political, economic, and social crises through emaciation of public institutions and disinvestment in much of the world's population, the question of how structurally abandoned individuals can cultivate a sense of unity and belonging is a pressing one.

13. Goffman described rights as the universal expectation that humans have to be perceived and treated in a positive way by relevant others.

14. As a comparison, for another research project in the same school, I interviewed twenty white students regarding their perceptions of school discipline and policing. Fourteen of them reported feeling that Latino students were treated more punitively. Four reported instances in which

a white student had committed an infraction, but a Latino student was blamed.

15. See Rios and Rodriguez (2011) for a political-economic analysis of this process that makes young people "incarcerable subjects." We argue that working-class young people are no longer "learning to labor" as Paul Willis (1977) suggested but "preparing for prison" as Paul Hirschfield (2009) would term it.

CHAPTER TWO

1. See Chambliss's classic study (1972) comparing differences in punishment for affluent white boys and impoverished white boys.

2. Cid Martinez (2016) brilliantly shows how local community institutions like the church and the gang—often more effectively than police—play instrumental roles in maintaining social order in the inner city.

3. Dick Hebdige, who studied delinquency in Britain, found that delinquents are torn between criminal and conventional behavior, but most of their beliefs mirror those of the adult law-abiding community.

CHAPTER THREE

1. Parts of this chapter were previously published in Victor Rios and Patrick Lopez-Aguado, "'Pelones y Matones': Chicano Cholos Perform for a Punitive Audience," in *Performing the US Latina and Latino Borderlands*, edited by Arturo J. Aldama, Chela Sandoval, and Peter Garcia (Bloomington: Indiana University Press, 2012), 382–401.

CHAPTER FOUR

1. An earlier version of this chapter was published in Victor Rios and Rachel Sarabia, "Synthesized Masculinities: The Mechanics of Manhood among Delinquent Boys," in *Exploring Masculinities: Identity, Inequality, Continuity and Change*, edited by C. J. Pascoe and Tristan Bridges (New York: Oxford University Press, 2016), 166–77. By permission of Oxford University Press. www.oup.com.

METHODOLOGICAL APPENDIX

1. The name of the city, youths' names, and other identifiers has been changed for protection purposes.

REFERENCES

Acuña, Rodolfo. 2004. *Occupied America: A History of Chicanos*. New York: Pearson Longman.

Adams, Rachel, and David Savran. 2002. *The Masculinities Studies Reader*. New Jersey: Wiley-Blackwell.

Ageton, Suzanne, and Elliot Delbert. 1974. "The Effect of Legal Processing on Delinquent Orientation." *Social Problems* 22:87–100.

Alkon, Alison Hope, and Christie Grace McCullen. 2011. "Whiteness and Farmers Markets: Performances, Perpetuations . . . Contestations?" *Antipode* 43, no. 4: 937–59.

Alexander, Michelle. 2013. *The New Jim Crow: Mass Incarceration in the Age of Colorblindness*. New York: The New Press.

Alfred, Taiaiake, and Jeff Corntassel. 2005. "Being Indigenous: Resurgences against Contemporary Colonialism." *Government and Opposition* 40, no. 4: 597–614.

Almaguer, Tomás. 1994. *Racial Fault Lines: The Historical Origins of White Supremacy in California*. Berkeley: University of California Press.

Alverman, Donna E., Kathleen A. Hinchman, David W. Moore, Stephan F. Phelps, and Diane R. Waff, eds. 2006. *Reconceptualizing the Literacies of Adolescents' Lives*. 2nd ed. Mahwah, NJ: Lawrence Erlbaum Associates.

Anderson, Elijah. 1990. *Streetwise: Race, Class, Change in an Urban Community*. Chicago: University of Chicago Press.

Anderson, Elijah. 1999. *Code of the Street: Decency, Violence, and Moral Life of the Inner City*. New York: Norton.

Anderson, Elijah. 2015. "The White Space." *Sociology of Race and Ethnicity* 1, no. 1: 10–21.

Babbie, Earl R. *The Practice of Social Research*, 9th ed. Belmont, CA: Wadsworth Thomson, 2001.

Barrera, Mario. 1979. *Race and Class in the Southwest*. Notre Dame, IN: University of Notre Dame Press.

Becker, Howard. 1963. *Outsiders: Studies in the Sociology of Deviance*. New York: Free Press.

Beckett, Katherine. 1997. *Making Crime Pay: Law and Order in Contemporary American Politics*. New York: Oxford University Press.

Bederman, Gail. 1996. *Manliness and Civilization: A Cultural History of Gender and Race in the United States*. Chicago: University of Chicago Press.

Bejarano, Cynthia. 2005. *Que Honda? Urban Youth Culture and Border Identity*. Tucson: University of Arizona Press.

Bonilla-Silva, Eduardo. 2006. *Racism without Racists: Color-Blind Racism and Racial Inequality in Contemporary America*. Lanham, MD: Rowman and Littlefield.

Boyles, A. S. 2015. *Race, Place, and Suburban Policing: Too Close for Comfort*. Berkeley: University of California Press.

Brotherton, David, and Luis Barrios. 2004. *The Almighty Latin King and Queen Nation: Street Politics and the Transformation of a New York City Gang*. New York: Columbia University Press.

Bouie, Jamelle. 2014. "Police Are Using Military Weapons to Occupy Ferguson, Missouri." *Slate*, August 13.

Bourdieu, Pierre. 1977. *Outline of a Theory of Practice*. Cambridge: Cambridge University Press.

Bourgois, Philippe. 1995. *In Search of Respect: Selling Crack in El Barrio*. New York: Cambridge University Press.

Bradley, Mike, and Lonnie Danchik. 1971. *Unbecoming Men: A Men's Consciousness-Raising Group Writes on Oppression and Themselves*. New York: Times Change Press.

Braithwaite, John. 1989. *Crime, Shame and Reintegration*. Cambridge: Cambridge University Press.

Burke, Peter J., and Jan E. Stets. 2009. "Identity Change." In *Identity Theory*. New York: Oxford Press.

Bynum, Timothy, Madeline Wordes, and Charles Corley. 1995. "Conceptions of Family and Juvenile Court Processes: A Qualitative Assessment." *Justice System Journal* 18, no. 2: 157–72.

Carbado, Devon W. 2002. "(E)racing the Fourth Amendment." *Michigan Law Review* 100, no. 5: 946–1044.

Carrigan, Tim, Bob Connel, and John Lee. 1985. "Toward A New Sociology of Masculinity." *Theory and Society* 14:551–604.

Carter, Prudence. 2005. *Keepin' It Real: School Success beyond Black and White*. Oxford: Oxford University Press.

Chambliss, William J. 1973. "The Saints and the Roughnecks." *Society* 11, no. 1: 24–31.

Charmaz, Kathy. 2002a. *Constructing Grounded Theory: A Practical Guide through Qualitative Analysis*. London: Sage.

Charmaz, Kathy. 2002b. "Qualitative Interviewing and Grounded Theory

Analysis." In *Handbook of Interview Research: Context and Method*, edited by J. Gubrium and J. A. Holstein, 675–93. Thousand Oaks, CA: Sage.

Chavez, Leo. 2008. *The Latino Threat: Constructing Immigrants, Citizens, and the Nation*. Stanford, CA: Stanford University Press.

Chesney-Lind, Meda, and Randall G. Shelden. 2004. *Girls, Delinquency, and Juvenile Justice*. 3rd ed. Belmont, CA: Wadsworth/Thomson Learning.

Clifford, J. 1986. "On Ethnographic Allegory." In *Writing Culture: The Poetics and Politics of Ethnography*, ed. J. Clifford and G. E. Marcus, 98–121. Berkeley: University of California Press.

Collins, Patricia Hill. 1986. "Learning from the Outsider Within: The Sociological Significance of Black Feminist Thought." *Social Problems* 33, no. 6: s14–s32.

Collins, Patricia Hill. 1998. "It's All in the Family: Intersections of Gender, Race, and Nation." *Hypatia* 13, no. 3: 62–82.

Comfort, Megan. 2008. *Doing Time Together: Love and Family in the Shadow of the Prison*. Chicago: University of Chicago Press.

Conchas, Gilberto, and James Diego Vigil. 2012. *Streetsmart Schoolsmart: Urban Poverty and the Education of Adolescent Boys*. New York: Teachers College Press.

Connel, Raewyn. 1987. *Gender and Power*. New Jersey: John Wiley and Sons.

Connell, R. W., and J. W. Messerchmidt. 2005. "Hegemonic Masculinity Rethinking the Concept." *Gender and Society* 19, no. 6.

Connell, Robert W. 1991. "Live Fast and Die Young: The Construction of Masculinity among Young Working-Class Men on the Margin of the Labour Market." *Journal of Sociology* 27, no. 2: 141–71.

Cooper, Frank. 2009. *Masculinities and the Law: A Multidimensional Approach*. New York: New York University Press.

Cosgrove, Denis. 1984. *Social Formation and Symbolic Landscape*. London: Croon Helm.

Coughlin, Brenda, and Alladi Venkatesh. 2003. "The Urban Street Gang After 1970." *Annual Review of Sociology* 29.

Covington, Jeannette. 1995. "Racial Classification in Criminology: The Reproduction of Racialized Crime." *Sociological Forum* 10:547–68.

Crenshaw, Kimberle. 1991. "Mapping the Margins: Intersectionality, Identity Politics, and Violence against Women of Color." *Stanford Law Review*, 1241–99.

Crowther, Chris. 2000. "Thinking about the 'Underclass': Towards a Political Economy of Policing." *Theoretical Criminology* 4, no. 2: 149–67.

Curry, David, and Irving Spergel. 1992. "Gang Involvement and Delinquency among Hispanic and African-American Adolescent Males." *Journal of Research in Crime and Delinquency* 29, no. 3: 273–91.

Dance, Jannelle. 2002. *Tough Fronts: The Impact of Street Culture on Schooling*. New York: Routledge Press.

Davis, Nanette J. 1999. *Youth Crisis: Growing Up in the High-Risk Society*. Westport, CT: Praeger.

Decker, Scott, and Barrik Van Winkle. 1996. *Life in the Gang: Family, Friends, and Violence*. New York: Cambridge University Press.

DeGenova, Nicholas. 2002. "Migrant Illegality and Deportability in Everyday Life." *Annual Review of Anthropology* 31:419–47.

Denzin, N. 1970. *The Research Act in Sociology*. London: Butterworth.

Devine, John F. 1996. *Maximum Security: The Culture of Violence in Inner-City Schools*. Chicago: University of Chicago Press.

Diaz-Cotto, Juanita. 2006. *Chicana Lives and Criminal Justice: Voices from El Barrio*. Austin: University of Texas Press.

Dodsworth, Francis. 2007. *Masculinity as Governance: Police, Public Service and the Embodiment of Authority, c. 1700–1850*.

DuBois, W. E. B. 2007. *The Souls of Black Folks* (1903). Oxford: Oxford University Press.

Duck, W. 2015. *No Way Out: Precarious Living in the Shadow of Poverty and Drug Dealing*. Chicago: University of Chicago Press.

Duneier, Mitch. 1992. *Slim's Table: Race, Respectability, and Masculinity*. Chicago: University of Chicago Press.

Duneier, Mitch. 1999. *Sidewalk*. New York: Farrar, Straus and Giroux.

Duneier, Mitchell, Philip Kasinitz, and Alexandra Murphy, eds. 2014. *The Urban Ethnography Reader*. Oxford: Oxford University Press.

Durán, Robert. 2013. *Gang Life in Two Cities: An Insider's Journey*. New York: Columbia University Press.

Durkheim, Émile. 1912. *The Elementary Forms of Religious Life*. Translated by Karen E. Fields. New York: Free Press.

Eason, John. 2016. *Big House on the Prairie: Rise of the Rural Ghetto and Prison Proliferation*. Chicago: University of Chicago Press.

Eder, Donna, and William Corsaro. 1999. "Ethnographic Studies of Children and Youth: Theoretical and Ethical Issues." *Journal of Contemporary Ethnography* 28, no. 5: 520–31.

Elder, Glen. 1985. *Life Course Dynamics: Trajectories and Transitions*. Ithaca, NY: Cornell University Press.

Emerson, Robert, Rachel Fretz, and Linda Shaw. 1995. *Writing Ethnographic Fieldnotes*. Chicago: University of Chicago Press.

Entwistle, J. 2001. *The Dressed Body*. Oxford: Berg.

Epp, C. R., S. Maynard-Moody, and D. P. Haider-Markel. 2014. *Pulled Over: How Police Stops Define Race and Citizenship*. Chicago: University of Chicago Press.

Evans, G. W. 2004. "The Environment of Childhood Poverty." *American Psychologist* 59, no. 2: 77.

Esbenson, Finn-Aage, and David Huizinga. 1993. "Gangs Drugs and Delinquency in a Survey of Urban Youth." *Criminology* 31, no. 3: 565–89.

Fader, Jamie. 2013. *Falling Back: Incarceration and Transitions to Adulthood among Urban Youth*. New Brunswick, NJ: Rutgers University Press.

Fagan, Jeffrey. 1990. "Social Processes of Delinquency and Drug Use among Urban Gangs." *Criminology* 27, no. 4: 183–219.

Fallik, S. W., and K. J. Novak. 2014. "Biased Policing." In *Encyclopedia of Criminology and Criminal Justice*, 154–62. New York: Springer.

Fanon, Frantz. 2008. *Black Skin, White Masks*. New York: Grove Press.

Feeley, Malcolm, and Jonathon Simon. 1992. "The New Penology: Notes on the Emerging Strategy of Corrections and Its Implications." *Criminology* 30:449–74.

Ferguson, Ann Arnett. 2000. *Bad Boys: Public Schools in the Making of Black Masculinity*. Ann Arbor: University of Michigan Press.

Flores, J. 2016. *Caught Up: Girls, Surveillance, and Wraparound Incarceration*. Berkeley: University of California Press.

Flores-Gonzalez, Nilda. 2002. *School Kids/Street Kids: Identity Development in Latino Students*. New York: Teacher's College Press.

Foucault, Michel. 1977. *Discipline and Punish: The Birth of the Prison*. Translated by Alan Sheridan. New York: Pantheon.

Gabbidon, Shaun, and Helen Greene. 2008. *Race and Crime*. Thousand Oaks, CA: Sage Publications.

Gans, Herbert J. 1962. *The Urban Villagers: Group and Class in the Life of Italian-Americans*. New York: Free Press.

Garland, David. 1997. "'Governmentality' and the Problem of Crime: Foucault, Criminology, Sociology." *Theoretical Criminology* 1, no. 2: 173–214.

Garland, David. 2001. *The Culture of Control: Crime and Social Order in Contemporary Society*. Chicago: University of Chicago Press.

Garot, Robert. 2010. *Who You Claim: Performing Gang Identity in School and on the Streets*. New York: New York Press.

Garot, Robert, and Jack Katz. 2003. "Provocative Looks: Gang Appearance and Dress Codes in an Inner-City Alternative School." *Ethnography* 4, no. 3: 421–54.

Gau, Jacinta, and Rod Brunson. 2010. "Procedural Justice and Order Maintenance Policing: A Study of Inner City Young Men's Perceptions of Police Legitimacy." *Justice Quarterly* 27, no. 2: 255–79.

Geertz, Clifford. 1973. *The Interpretation of Cultures: Selected Essays*. New York: Basic Books Publisher.

Giddens, Anthony 1979. *Central Problems in Social Theory: Action, Structure, and Contradiction in Social Analysis*. Berkeley: University of California Press.

Giddens, Anthony. 1984. *The Constitution of Society: Outline of the Theory of Structuration*. Berkeley: University of California Press.

Giroux, H. A. 2013. *America's Education Deficit and the War on Youth: Reform beyond Electoral Politics*. New York: NYU Press.

Glaser, Barney, and Anslem Strauss. 1967. *The Discovery of Grounded Theory: Strategies for Qualitative Research*. Chicago: Aldine Publishing Company.

Goffman, Alice. 2009. "On the Run: Wanted Men in a Philadelphia Ghetto." *American Sociological Review* 74, no. 2: 339–57.

Goffman, Alice. 2014. *On the Run: Fugitive Life in an American City*. Chicago: University of Chicago Press.

Goffman, E. 1989. "On Fieldwork." *Journal of Contemporary Ethnography* 18, no. 2: 123–32.

Goffman, Erving. 1990. *Stigma: Notes on the Management of Spoiled Identity*. London: Penguin Books.

Hagan, John, and Holly Foster. 2006. "Profiles of Punishment and Privilege: Secret and Disputed Deviance during the Racialized Transition to American Adulthood." *Crime, Law and Social Change* 46, nos. 1–2: 65–85.

Hagedorn, John. 1988. *People and Folks: Gangs, Crime, and the Underclass in a Rustbelt City*. Chicago: Lake View Press.

Hahn, Harlan. 1971. "Police in Urban Society." *American Behavioral Scientists* 16, no. 3.

Hall, Stuart, Chas Critcher, Tony Jefferson, and John N. Clarke. 1978. *Policing the Crisis: Mugging, the State, and Law and Order*. New York: Holmes and Meier.

Hannerz, Ulf. 2004. *Soulside: Inquiries into Ghetto Culture and Community*. Chicago: University of Chicago Press.

Harding, David. 2010. *Living the Drama: Community, Conflict, and Culture among Inner-City Boys*. Chicago: University of Chicago Press.

Harris, A. P. 2000. "Gender, Violence, Race, and Criminal Justice." *Stanford Law Review*, 777–807.

Harris, Alexes, and Walter Allen. 2003. "Lest We Forget Thee . . . : The

Under- and Over-Representation of Black and Latino Youth in California Higher Education and Juvenile Justice Institutions." *Race and Society* 6, no. 2: 99–123.

Hartigan, John. 1999. *Racial Situations: Class Predicaments of Whiteness in Detroit*. Princeton, NJ: Princeton University Press.

Hartsock, N. C. 1983. "The Feminist Standpoint: Developing the Ground for a Specifically Feminist Historical Materialism." In *Discovering Reality*, 283–310. Springer Netherlands.

Hepburn, J. R. 1977. "The Impact of Police Intervention upon Juvenile Delinquents." *Criminology* 15:235–62.

Herbert, Steve. 2006. *Citizens, Cops, and Power: Recognizing the Limits of Community*. Chicago: University of Chicago Press.

Hirschfield, P. 2009. "Another Way Out: The Impact of Juvenile Arrests on High School Dropout." *Sociology of Education* 82, no. 4: 368–93.

Hodkinson, Paul. 2005. "'Insider Research' in the Study of Youth Cultures." *Journal of Youth Studies* 8, no. 2: 131–49.

Hooks, B., 1994. *Outlaw Culture: Resisting Representations*. New York: Routledge.

Horowitz, Ruth. 1983. *Honor and the American Dream: Culture and Identity in a Chicano Community*. New Brunswick, NJ: Rutgers University Press.

Huizinga, D., and F. Esbensen. 1993. "Examining Developmental Trajectories in Delinquency Using Accelerated Longitudinal Research Designs." *Cross-National Longitudinal Research on Human Development and Criminal Behavior* 74.

Jankowski, Martin. 1991. *Islands in the Street: Gangs and American Urban Society*. Berkeley: University of California Press.

Kataoka, S. H., L. Zhang, and K. B. Wells. 2002. "Unmet Need for Mental Health Care among US Children: Variation by Ethnicity and Insurance Status." *American Journal of Psychiatry* 159, no. 9: 1548–55.

Kelley, Robin D. G. 1997. *Yo' Mama's Disfunktional! Fighting the Culture Wars in Urban America*. Boston: Beacon.

Kennedy, D. M. 2009. *Deterrence and Crime Prevention: Reconsidering the Prospect of Sanction*, vol. 2. New York: Routledge.

Kimmel, Michael. 1993. "Masculinity as Homophobia: Fear Shame, and Silence in the Construction of Gender Identity."

Kimmel, Michael. 2003. *Men and Masculinities: A Social, Cultural, and Historical Encyclopedia*. Santa Barbara, CA: ABC-Clio.

Kimmel, Michael, and Matthew Mahler. 2003. "Adolescent Masculinity, Homophobia and Violence." *American Behavioral Scientists* 46, no. 10: 1439–58.

Klein, M. W., and C. L. Maxson. 2010. *Street Gang Patterns and Policies.* Oxford: Oxford University Press.

Kupchik, A., and G. Ward. 2013. "Race, Poverty, and Exclusionary School Security: An Empirical Analysis of US Elementary, Middle, and High Schools." *Youth Violence and Juvenile Justice,* 1541204013503890.

Lemert, Edwin. 1951. *Social Pathology: A Systematic Approach to the Theory of Sociopathic Behavior.* New York: McGraw Hill Press.

Lopez, Nancy. 2002. *Hopeful Girls, Troubled Boys: Race and Gender Disparity in Urban Education.* London: Routledge.

Lopez-Aguado, P. 2013. "Working between Two Worlds: Gang Intervention and Street Liminality." *Ethnography* 14, no. 2: 186–206.

MacLeod, Jay. 2008. *Ain't No Makin' It: Aspirations and Attainment in a Low-Income Neighborhood.* Boulder, CO: Westview.

Martin, Susan 1999. "Police Force or Police Service? Gender and Emotional Labor." *Annals of the American Academy of Political and Social Science* 561:111–26.

Martinez, C. 2016. *The Neighborhood Has Its Own Rules: Latinos and African Americans in South Los Angeles.* New York: NYU Press.

Marx, Gary T. 1981. "Ironies of Social Control: Authorities as Contributors to Deviance through Escalation, Nonenforcement and Covert Facilitation." *Social Problems* 28, no. 3: 221–46.

Matza, David. 1964. *Delinquency and Drift: From the Research Program of the Center for the Study of Law and Society.* Berkeley: University of California Press.

Mendoza-Denton, Norma. 2008. *Homegirls: Language and Cultural Practice among Latina Youth Gangs.* Hoboken, NJ: Wiley-Blackwell.

Menjivar, Cecilia, and Daniel Kanstroom. 2013. *Constructing Immigrant "Illegality": Critiques, Experiences, and Responses.* Cambridge: Cambridge University Press.

Messerschmidt, J. W. 1993. *Masculinities and Crime: Critique and Reconceptualization of Theory.* Lanham, MD: Rowman & Littlefield Publishers.

Messerschmidt, James. 1999. *Nine Lives: Adolescent Masculinities, The Body and Violence.* Boulder, CO: Westview Press.

Meyerhoff, Barbara, and Jay Ruby. 1982. "Introduction: Reflexivity and Its Relatives." In *A Crack in the Mirror: Reflexive Perspectives in Anthropology,* edited by Jay Ruby, 1–38. Philadelphia: University of Pennsylvania Press.

Miller, J. A. 1995. "Struggles over the Symbolic: Gang Style and the Meanings of Social Control." *Cultural Criminology,* 213–34.

Morgan, P. L., J. Staff, M. M. Hillemeier, G. Farkas, and S. Maczuga. 2013.

"Racial and Ethnic Disparities in ADHD Diagnosis from Kindergarten to Eighth Grade." *Pediatrics*, peds-2012.

Newman, K. S., 1999. *No Shame in My Game: The Working Poor in the Inner City*. New York: Vintage.

Newton, Lina. 2008. *Illegal, Alien, or Immigrant: The Politics of Immigration Reform*. New York: New York University Press.

Ngai, Mae. 2014. *Impossible Subjects: Illegal Aliens and the Making of Modern America*. Princeton, NJ: Princeton University Press.

Obama, Barack. 2004. Democratic National Convention speech. Transcribed in "Illinois Senate Candidate Barack Obama: FDCH E-Media," *Washington Post*, July 27.

Olguin, Ben. 1997. "Tattoos, Abjection, and the Political Unconscious: Towards A Semiotics of the Pinto Visual Vernacular." *Cultural Critique* 37: 159–213.

Omi, Michael, and Howard Winant. 1994. *Racial Formation in the United States: From the 1960s to the 1990s*. New York: Routledge.

Pager, D. 2007. "The Use of Field Experiments for Studies of Employment Discrimination: Contributions, Critiques, and Directions for the Future." *Annals of the American Academy of Political and Social Science* 609, no. 1: 104–33.

Parenti, Christian. 2000. *Lockdown America: Police and Prisons in the Age of Crisis*. London: Verso.

Pascoe, C. J. 2011. *Dude, You're A Fag: Masculinity and Sexuality in High School*. Berkeley: University of California Press.

Patillo-McCoy, Mary. 1999. *Black Picket Fences: Privilege and Peril among the Black Middle Class*. Chicago: University of Chicago Press.

Payne, Yasser A. 2006. "A Gangster and a Gentleman: How Street Life Oriented U.S. Born African Men Negotiate Issues of Survival in Relation to Their Masculinity." *Men and Masculinity* 8, no. 3: 288–97.

Pyke K. D. 1996. "Class-Based Masculinities: The Interdependence of Gender, Class, and Interpersonal Power." *Gender and Society* 10, no. 5: 527–49.

Rios, V. M. 2009. "The Consequences of the Criminal Justice Pipeline on Black and Latino Masculinity." *Annals of the American Academy of Political and Social Science* 623, no. 1: 150–62.

Rios, V. M. 2011. *Punished: Policing the Lives of Black and Latino Boys*. New York: New York University Press.

Rios, V. M. 2015a. *On the Run: Fugitive Life in an American City*. By Alice Goffman.

Rios, V. M. 2015b. "Decolonizing the White Space in Urban Ethnography." *City & Community* 14, no. 3: 258–61.

Rios, V. M., and C. Rodriguez. 2011. "Incarcerable Subjects." In *Young Men in Uncertain Times*, 241.

Robinson, W. I., and M. Barrera. 2012. "Global Capitalism and Twenty-First Century Fascism: A US Case Study." *Race & Class* 53, no. 3: 4–29.

Rodriguez, Luis. 2005. *Always Running: La Vida Loca Gang Days in LA*. New York: Simon and Schuster.

Sabo, D. F., T. A. Kupers, and W. J. London. 2001. *Prison Masculinities*. Philadelphia: Temple University Press.

Sánchez-Jankowski, Martín. 1991. *Islands in the Street: Gangs and American Urban Society*. Berkeley: University of California Press.

Schneider, A., and H. Ingram. 1993. "Social Construction of Target Populations: Implications for Politics and Policy." *American Political Science Review* 87, no. 2: 334–47.

Schuman, Rebecca. 2014. "The Birth of the #Ferguson Syllabus in American Colleges." *Slate*, September 8.

Siegler, Kirk. 2014. "For LAPD Cop Working Skid Row, 'There's Always Hope.'" *All Things Considered*. National Public Radio, October 14. http://www.npr.org/2014/10/14/353525565/for-lapd-cop-working-skid-row-theres-always-hope.

Small, Mario Luis. 2004. *Villa Victoria: The Transformation of Social Capital in a Boston Barrio*. Chicago: University of Chicago Press.

Small, Mario Luis. 2015. "De-Exoticizing Ghetto Poverty: On the Ethics of Representation in Urban Ethnography." *City and Community* 14 (December): 4.

Small, Mario Luis, David Harding, and Michelle Lamont. 2010. "Reconsidering Culture and Poverty." *Social Science Research Network*.

Smith, L. T. 1999. *Decolonizing Methodologies: Research and Indigenous Peoples*. New York: Zed Books.

Snow, David A., and Leon Anderson. 1987. "Identity Work among the Homeless: The Verbal Construction and Avowal of Personal Identities." *American Journal of Sociology* 92, no. 6: 1336–71.

Sollund, Ragnhild. 2006. "Racialization in Police Stop and Search Practice." *Critical Criminology* 14, no. 13: 265–92.

Strauss, Anselm. 1987. *Qualitative Analysis for Social Scientists*. Cambridge: Cambridge University Press.

Sudnow, David. 1978. *Ways of Hand: The Organization of Improvised Conduct*. Cambridge, MA: MIT Press.

Sullivan, Mercer. 2005. "Maybe We Shouldn't Study 'Gangs': Does Reification Obscure Youth Violence?" *Journal of Contemporary Criminal Justice* 21, no. 2.

Swidler, Ann. 1986. "Culture in Action: Symbols and Strategies." *American Sociological Review* 51, no. 2: 273–86.

Thornberry, T. P. 1998. *Membership in Youth Gangs and Involvement in Serious and Violent Juvenile Offenders: Risk Factors and Successful Interventions.* Thousand Oaks, CA: Sage Publications.

Tseng, V., and E. Seidman. 2007. "A Systems Framework for Understanding Social Settings." *American Journal of Community Psychology* 39, nos. 3–4: 217–28.

Van Cleve, N. 2016. *Crook County: Racism and Injustice in America's Largest Criminal Court.* Stanford, CA: Stanford University Press.

Venkatesh, Sudhir Alladi. 2008. *Gang Leader for a Day: A Rogue Sociologist Takes to the Streets.* New York: Penguin.

Vigil, James Diego. 1988. *Barrio Gangs: Street Life and Identity in Southern California.* Austin: University of Texas Press.

Vigil, James Diego. 2002. *A Rainbow of Gangs: Street Culture in the Mega-City.* Austin: University of Texas Press.

Vigil, James Diego. 2007. *The Projects: Gang and Non-Gang Families in East Los Angeles.* Austin: University of Texas Press.

Vigil, James Diego. 2010. *Barrio Gangs: Street Life and Identity in Southern California.* Austin: University of Texas Press.

Wacquant, Loic. 2002. "Scrutinizing the Street: Poverty, Morality, and the Pitfalls of Urban Ethnography." *American Journal of Sociology* 107, no. 6: 1468–532.

Wacquant, Loic. 2009. *Punishing the Poor: The Neoliberal Government of Social Insecurity.* Durham, NC: Duke University Press.

West, Candace, and Sarah Fenstemaker. 1995. "Doing Difference." *Gender and Society* 9, no. 1.

Widdicombe, Sue, and Robin Wooffitt. 1995. *The Language of Youth Subcultures: Social Identity in Action.* New York: Harvester Wheatsheaf.

Wielder, Lawrence, and Steven Pratt. 1989. *On Being a Recognizable Indian among Indians.* Hillsdale, NJ: Lawrence Erlbaum Associates.

Willis, Paul E. 1977. *Learning to Labour: How Working Class Kids Get Working Class Jobs.* Farnborough, UK: Saxon House.

Wilson, J. Q., and G. L. Kelling. 1982. "Broken Windows." In *Critical Issues in Policing: Contemporary Readings,* 395–407.

Wordes, M., and T. S. Bynum. 1995. "Policing Juveniles: Is There Bias against Youths of Color." *Minorities in Juvenile Justice,* 47–65.

Yoshino, Kenji. 2006. *Covering: The Hidden Assault on Our Civil Rights*. New York: Random House Trade Paperbacks.

Young, Alford, Jr. 2006. *The Minds of Marginalized Black Men: Making Sense of Mobility, Opportunity, and Future Life Chances*. Princeton, NJ: Princeton University Press.

INDEX

ADHD. *See* attention deficit/hyper-activity disorder
African Americans: cultural framing and, 22–23, 159, 176 (*see also* cultural frames); dichotomy and, 8, 185n5; marginalization and, 6, 72; masculinity and, 109 (*see also* masculinity); police and, 12–13, 162, 185n2 (*see also* police); punitive culture and, 6; racism and (*see* racism); whites and (*see* whites); women, 188n20 (*see also* women). *See also specific topics*
aggression. *See* violence
alcohol, 62, 65, 93, 100, 120, 149, 189n6
Alkon, Alison Hope, 186n11
allegory, ethnography and, 177
alternative school. *See* continuation school
Anderson, Elijah, 110, 175
Anglo culture. *See* whites
archaeology, ethnographic, 11
at-risk label, 7, 31, 76, 89, 149, 154, 156, 185n6
attention deficit/hyperactivity disorder (ADHD), 31, 189n4
authority figures, 27, 33–34, 39, 148, 153; cholo style and, 41–42, 84, 90 (*see also* cholo subculture); contradictions and, 42; control and, 11–12, 36, 43; counterresistance in, 63; cultural frames and (*see* cultural frames); cultural recognition and, 54, 71–73, 159–62 (*see also* cultural misrecognition); dress and, 83 (*see also* dress); gang members as, 45–46, 65; institutions and (*see* institutions); interactions with, 6, 22–23, 26–27, 36, 63, 72, 78, 85, 154, 157, 158,

171; masculinity and, 102, 104, 110 (*see also* masculinity); pernicious fire and, 11–14; police (*see* police); power and, 130; prison and, 69 (*see also* prisons); researcher and, 61, 63; respected, 33; targeting and, 59, 63 (*see also* targeting). *See also specific types, topics*

Barrios, Luis, 22
Boyle, Andrea, 185n2
Boyle, Greg, 164
Brotherton, David, 22
Brown, Michael, 12

CalGang database, 20. *See also* databases
Californio identity, 29–30, 189n2
care, culture of, 155–81
case-workers, 163. *See also specific topics*
CCC. *See* Civilian Conservation Core
Chambliss, William J., 191n1
check-ins, 120, 121
Chicago school, 174
cholo subculture, 75–77, 79, 81; appeal of, 80; criminality and, 75, 76, 87; cultural frame of, 84; defined, 75; dress, 17, 35–37, 51–52, 79, 82–86, 87, 90, 128; identity and, 80, 93; marginality, viii, 93; masculinity (*see* masculinity); public events, 84; resistance and, 80, 81, 82, 84, 85; risks and, 93; street culture and (*see* street culture). *See also specific topics*
church, 17, 80, 175, 191n2
Civilian Conservation Core (CCC), 163, 164
class, 16, 17, 30, 186n12
Clifford, James, 177